ABORTION

ABORTION

Statutes, Policies, and Public Attitudes the World Over

Rita J. Simon

PRAEGER

Westport, Connecticut
London

Library of Congress Cataloging-in-Publication Data

Simon, Rita James.
Abortion : statutes, policies, and public attitudes the world over / Rita J. Simon.
p. cm.
Includes bibliographical references and index.
ISBN 0–275–96060–9 (hardcover : alk. paper). — ISBN 0–275–96061–7 (pbk. : alk. paper)
1. Abortion—Government policy—Cross-cultural studies.
2. Abortion—Law and legislation—Cross-cultural studies.
3. Abortion—Public opinion—Cross-cultural studies. I. Title.
HQ767.S448 1998
363.46—dc21 98–14928

British Library Cataloguing in Publication Data is available.

Library of Congress Catalog Card Number: 98–14928
ISBN: 0–275–96060–9 (hc)
0–275–96061–7 (pbk.)

First published in 1998

Praeger Publishers, 88 Post Road West, Westport, CT 06881
An imprint of Greenwood Publishing Group, Inc.

Printed in the United States of America

The paper used in this book complies with the Permanent Paper Standard issued by the National Information Standards Organization (Z39.48–1984).

10 9 8 7 6 5 4 3 2 1

Contents

Introduction

Abortion: Statutes, Policies, and Public Attitudes the World Over is the first in a series of volumes that examines a major public policy issue using an explicitly comparative approach. The organizing focus of the series is the analysis of important social issues about which most societies in the world have enacted laws and statutes, and about which most of their members have opinions that they voice in the public arena. These are issues that receive extensive media as well as legislative and judicial attention. Following the abortion issue, subsequent topics are likely to include, euthanasia, marriage and divorce, inheritance, drugs, and public education. Each volume will report laws and statutes adopted by the countries included, public opinion surveys, media coverage of the debates surrounding the adoption of new statutes, and data on the number of and grounds for abortions, adoptions, divorces, etc., per annum. The countries included will be represented by their geographic as well as political, ethnic, and religious characteristics. Thus, the United States, Canada, a sample of Western and Eastern European countries, Muslim countries, African and Latin American countries, Australia, and among Asian countries Japan, China, and India will be included. Each volume will serve as a handbook that contains basic empirical data and comprehensive references on a social issue or practice under study worldwide. Abortion is the first venture.

Following a brief historical introduction, the major section of this volume is divided into (1) a report on the legal statutes pertaining to abortion in the selective countries and (2) an account of public attitudes toward abortion based on responses to national public opinion polls. There is also a discussion of the relationships between the laws and statutes pertaining to abortion and the nations' policies vis-à-vis population growth and control.

ABORTION

1

Historical Background

Induced abortion is the termination of unwanted pregnancy by destruction of the fetus. It is one of the oldest methods of fertility control and one of the most widely used. It has been and is practiced in all regions of the world.

Every society has passed laws or established policies concerning induced abortions. Those laws and policies are usually a product of the legal heritage of the country as well as the social, political, economic, and religious values and institutions of the society.

In preliterate societies a woman whose pregnancy is unacceptable to the community, a woman who has broken its rules about appropriate sexual partners or the number of children, a pregnant widow, an unmarried girl or a girl too young, a woman who has had sexual intercourse with an outsider or whose pregnancy is the result of an adulterous relationship is expected to have an abortion. There is no judgment attached to the abortion itself, but there are usually strong moral judgments about the pregnancy and the conditions that led to it.

Going back in history and examining the laws and policies vis-à-vis abortion reveals that in ancient Greek and Roman societies an induced abortion was considered a crime against the husband. The earliest Christian views on abortion may be found in a second-century letter written by Barnabas, a follower of Saint Paul, which states: "Thou shalt not kill the fetus by an abortion or commit infanticide." Saint Basil the Great of the Eastern Church wrote in 376 A.D. "A woman who deliberately destroys a fetus is answerable for murder."

The first systematic attempt to organize ecclesiastical legislation occurred in 1140. The laws stated: "He is not a murderer who bring about abortion before the soul is in the body." But twelfth-century Canon Law considered abortion homicide if it was performed after quickening (movement of the fetus), which was assumed to take place forty days after conception for the male fetus and eighty days after conception for the female fetus. According to John T. Noonan, Catholic theology "treated the embryo's life as less than absolute, but only the value of the mother's life was given greater weight." Except for a brief period in the mid-sixteenth century, when abortion could be punished by excommunication, the view that abortion was not a punishable act if it occurred in early pregnancy was held by the Christian Church until 1869, when Pope Pius IX decreed that quickening takes place at conception and that for Roman Catholics, the punishment for abortion was excommunication. The Second Vatican Council under Pope John XXIII stated that from the moment of conception life must be guarded with the greatest care, while abortion and infanticide are unspeakable crimes.

Turning to secular law, we find that early English Common Law also made a distinction between early and late abortion, drawing the dividing line at quickening. Prior to 1803, abortion before quickening was not considered a crime, and even abortion later in pregnancy was not severely punished. In 1803, the first secular law concerning abortion was passed in England, the Irish Chalky Act. The Irish Chalky Act punished a woman who obtained an abortion by life imprisonment. The Chalky Act was followed by the Offenses Against the Person Act passed in 1861. That act stated: "It is a felony punishable by life imprisonment for any woman with child unlawfully to procure or attempt to procure her own miscarriage and for any other person to do any similar act with similar intent whether she be with child or not." The Offences Against the Person Act of 1861 formed the basis for abortion law throughout the Commonwealth.

In Civil Law, the first widely adopted statute concerning induced abortion was written into the Napoleonic Code of 1810. It prescribed harsh sentences for any woman who procured an abortion and for any person who performed an abortion.

Another set of "religious laws" applicable in Muslim countries also had important implications for abortion policies. Islamic law is contained in the Koran and the Sunna, a collection of acts and statements made by the Prophet and by scholarly interpretation. Although the different schools of Islamic law (Sunni and Shiah, for example) differ somewhat in their interpretations, Islamic law forbids the killing of the soul. The different schools of Islamic law disagree when a fetus acquires a soul. Some declare the time as 40 days after conception and others as 120 days. Some schools permit abortions prior to quickening if there are justifiable grounds, others forbid abortions even before quickening. Islamic law, generally, permits abortion when the pregnancy endangers the mother's life, regardless of the duration of gestation.

Even though leaders of the American Jewish community and especially Jewish women have been among the most vocal supporters of a "woman's right to chose," the traditional Jewish position derived from the body of law in the Talmud is that "the unborn fetus is to all intents and purposes a person and is entitled to the protection of society. Fetal life is a form of human life and is entitled to the self-same safeguards and protections which society accords to all its members." Under Orthodox principles abortion is permissible only to save the life of the mother. Abortion is not permissible for the sake of destroying a defective child unless and only if it is essential to the preservation of the physical and mental health of the mother.

In the State of Israel, abortion is permissible to protect the mother's physical and mental health, if the fetus is impaired, or if the mother was the victim of rape or incest. The reasoning underlying the latter two criteria is that to allow the pregnancy to continue would be threatening to the mother's mental and physical well being.

The possibility of abortion was written out of Canon Law in 1917 even if the pregnancy endangered the mother's life. A major change in English Common Law following the act of 1861 occurred in 1938 when the judge in the case of *Rex v. Bourne* specified instances when an abortion would be lawful. In the *Bourne* case, a physician was accused of performing an abortion on a 14 year old who had been raped. Dr. Aleck Bourne was acquitted on the grounds that continuation of the pregnancy would have caused the girl to become a "mental wreck." The judge declared that the words "unlawfully" in the 1861 act implied that abortion performed with the intent of preserving the woman's life or health was not a criminal act and that health included both physical and mental health.

Changes made in the French Civil Law in 1920 and 1923 changed abortion from a crime to a misdemeanor, with reduced sentences.

In November 1920, in the newly formed Union of Soviet Socialist Republic, Lenin passed the first liberal abortion law in Europe. Abortion under hospital conditions was legalized. The law was adopted on the basis of female equality and in recognition of a woman's right to control her own fertility. But in 1935, the law was revised and in June 1936, the Council of the People's Commissions decided to forbid the performance of abortion, except when the mother's life was at stake or there was evidence of inherited disease. Violations were to be punished by two to three years imprisonment. In 1944 all legal abortion was abolished and persons who aided women in securing an abortion were sentenced to two years of imprisonment. A major impetus for the change in policy from pro to antiabortion was the state's and the Communist Party's concern that the country's population growth was declining. Stalin saw population growth as increasingly important for a strong militarized society.

In 1955, the Soviet government reversed itself again and enacted legislation that legalized abortion on the earlier Leninist grounds that no woman should be forced to bear a child she did not want, and because a large number of abortions were being performed illegally under unsanitary conditions and maternal death was very high. The laws that permitted abortion that were enacted in the Soviet Union in 1955 were also enacted in the countries in the "Soviet Bloc" (Bulgaria, Hungary, Poland, Romania, etc.).

Elsewhere in Europe, abortions also remained illegal, although with the onset of the worldwide depression in the 1930s, the number of abortions increased drastically. When the National Socialist Party gained power in Germany in 1932, Hitler announced: "The use of contraception means a violation of nature, a degradation of womanhood, motherhood and love. Nazi ideals demand that the practice of abortion shall be exterminated with a strong hand." In 1936, in response to attacks from international feminist movements and liberal Western governments, Hitler declared: "I am often told, 'you want to force women out of professions.' No, I only want to create to the greatest extent the possibility of founding a family and having children because our folk needs them above all things." Women supporters of the Nazi Party agreed with Hitler and stated: ". . . the only work of the German woman is to serve the German male—'to minister in the home' attending to 'the care of man, soul, body and mind' continuously 'from the first to the last moment of man's existence.' " Family planning clinics were closed and prison sentences from six to fifteen years were imposed on doctors who performed abortions. In 1943, legislation was passed making abortion a capital offense.

In Italy, the Fascist government also passed anticontraceptive and antiabortion legislation. Under the Vichy government of France during World War II, Marshall Henri Phillippe Petain passed a law that made abortion a capital offense.

In the earliest period of American history, abortion was viewed primarily as a recourse for women who wanted to rid themselves of pregnancies that resulted from illicit relationships. But by the end of the eighteenth century, birth rates exceeded any recorded in Europe. With the rapid increase in birth rates, there was also a sharp rise in the incidence of abortions. By the midcentury, reports were published that stated American women were aborting at least one in five pregnancies.

Most women practicing abortions were married, white, and native born. Most Americans did not consider a pre-quickened fetus a distinct human being with a separate existence of its own. The "quickening" doctrine remained in effect in every jurisdiction in the United States as late as 1860. This standard or criterion was essentially unchanged from British and Colonial Common Law. Under this doctrine, the performance of an abortion, provided it took place prior to quickening and provided the woman was not injured, was not an indictable action.

In the United States, it was the nation's doctors who launched and organized a major campaign to stamp out what they referred to as an "abortion epidemic." The campaign was organized under the auspices of the American Medical Association. The campaign persuaded many state legislatures to drop quickening rules from their criminal code and to revoke common law immunities for women undergoing abortions. The effect was to proscribe most, but not all, types of abortions as illegal actions that carry legal penalties. Many of the statutes passed by the separate states during the post–Civil War period remained unchanged for more than a century. Those laws established the official policies toward the practice of abortion that prevailed until the Supreme Court handed down its decision in *Roe v. Wade* in 1972.

While the British Common Law doctrine on abortion spread to and influenced the Canadian, American, Australian, and other former British colonies, the Code Napoleon adopted in France in 1810 spread through the French colonies and into Latin America, Asia, and Middle Eastern countries, such as Thailand, Japan, and Iran, that had never been part of the French empire.

Mary Ann Glendon, in *Abortion and Divorce in Western Law*, argues that countries may apply the same criteria for permitting or proscribing abortion but the principles or values that underlie those criteria may be quite different. For example, Glendon states that what American law about abortion communicates is that fetal "potential life" is outweighed by any interest of the pregnant woman until the last trimester. Even then, fetal life need not be protected as a constitutional matter. But, she claims, in contrast all of the Western European law, while permitting abortion on a wide variety of grounds, communicates that fetal life is an important interest of the society and that abortion is not a substitute for birth control.

United States law, according to Glendon, stresses autonomy, separation, and isolation vis-à-vis family matters whereas Western European countries such as Sweden emphasize sexual equality and social solidarity; West Germany, social solidarity and prolife; and France, equality, life, and solidarity. Americans think of abortion issues as involving rights, either the right to life of the fetus or a woman's right to privacy, choice, or control over her own body. European laws emphasize communitarian values. They also emphasize the interests that a society as a whole has, not only in the abortion decision, but in the long range formation of benefits and attitudes about human life.

The next chapter describes in detail the criteria or lack of them that permit abortion in a wide range of countries that embody common and civil law traditions as well as religious law and what remains of socialist law.

2

Abortion Statutes in Selective Countries Worldwide

This chapter reports the current abortion statutes in a sample of countries in Western and Eastern Europe, Asia, Australia, Africa, the Middle East, Latin and Central America, and North America.[1] It also provides information about the history and background of those statutes, the criteria employed, the conditions surrounding their implementation (i.e., does the government pay for legal abortions?), the punishments for violation of the statutes, and wherever possible, data on the number of abortions reported annually. The next chapter assesses public support for the statutes by examining national poll data in thirty-one countries.

WESTERN EUROPE

The countries included here are France, Germany, Austria, the Netherlands, Denmark, Sweden, United Kingdom, Ireland, Italy, and Spain.

France

Current criteria for abortion in France are based on a statute passed in 1975, and amended in 1979 and again in 1982. An abortion may be performed before the end of the tenth week for the following reasons: the fetus is impaired, the woman has been raped or is the victim of incest, or the preservation of the woman's mental or physical health is at risk. The abortion must be performed by a physician in an approved hospital. The government covers 70 percent of the cost associated with the care and hospitalization associated with the lawful abortion. Beyond the tenth week, an abortion may be performed only when the pregnancy poses a grave danger to the woman's health or on eugenic grounds. Two physicians must attest to the woman's health risk. A woman who obtains an abortion in violation of these rules or induces one herself is subject to prison for six months to two years and may be fined 360 to 20,000 francs. A person who performs an illegal abortion with or without the woman's consent may be imprisoned for one to five years and fined from 1800 to 100,000 francs.

In 1988, RU486, an abortion pill, was approved for sale and distribution in France. The Ministry of Health closely regulates its use. For example, the drug cannot be used after the forty-ninth day of amenorrhoea. It must be taken in the presence of a physician and the patient must be examined by a physician forty-eight hours afterwards to be administered prostaglandin, and one week later to verify the termination of pregnancy. Currently, about one-fourth of all legal abortions employ RU486.

In 1988, the abortion rate was 13.2 per 1000 women from 15 to 44 years of age. From 1976 to 1988, the rates ranged from 12.3 in 1976 to 15.9 in 1981. In 1997, experts reported that 250,000 legal abortions were performed annually. They also estimated that about 5000 women go abroad, usually to Great Britain, the Netherlands, and Spain for abortions after they are ten weeks into their pregnancy.

Germany

Abortion law was one of the more complex issues that had to be resolved following the unification of West and East Germany. Finally in June 1992, the Parliament adopted the current law that permits abortion if the mother's physical or mental health is in danger, if she is the victim of rape or incest, or if there is some impairment of the fetus. Under "exceptional circumstances," according to a federal constitutional decision handed down in May 1993, an abortion may be granted for economic, social, or often personal reasons. But abortions that are performed for other than medical, eugenic, or ethical reasons are not subsidized under the compulsory health insurance program. And women who seek an abortion for other than medical reasons must attend a pre-abortion social counseling session with a physician.

Prior to unification, the abortion rates per 1000 women 15 to 44 years of age ranged from 1.5 in 1975 to 5.8 in 1990 in the Federal Republic of Germany and from 25.2 to 20.1 for the same time span in the German Democratic Republic. In 1991, the abortion rate in the unified Germany was 8.7 per 1000 women 15 to 44 years of age. In 1995, nearly 3000 women were reported to have traveled to the Netherlands for an abortion.

Austria

Abortion was decriminalized in 1974 and made available on request during the first trimester of pregnancy after medical consultation. An abortion may be performed after the first trimester if necessary to avert serious danger to the woman's life or health, if there is suspicion of fetal impairment, or if the woman is a minor. All abortions must be performed by a licensed physician. The government subsidizes only those abortions performed on medical grounds.

The Netherlands

In 1981, a law was passed that repealed the nineteenth century statutes that severely restricted abortion. Currently abortion is permitted virtually upon request up to thirteen weeks of gestation. There is a five-day waiting period between the time a woman has her initial consultation and the abortion is performed. The cost is subsidized by the government. But the same 1981 law also states that hospitals that do not wish to perform abortions on grounds of conscience may apply for exemptions. Article 20 of the same statute also exempts physicians from being forced to perform an induced abortion if it is against their beliefs.

The number of foreign patients seeking abortions, especially later term abortions, reached as high as 90 percent of all abortions requested in some clinics in Holland in 1997. In 1989, the abortion rate was 9.7 per 1000 live births.

Denmark

Until 1939 abortion was illegal except if a woman's life was in danger. In 1973, the laws were changed to what they are currently. Abortion up to the end of the first trimester is available on demand. After twelve weeks, a woman seeking an abortion must gain the authorization of a committee composed of a social worker and two doctors. Having an abortion after twelve weeks without such authorization is punishable by up to two years in prison.

Between 1970 and 1987 the abortion rates per 1000 women 15 to 45 years of age increased from 9.4 to 18.3. Single women and those under 20 years of age have the highest abortion rates.

Sweden

At the beginning of the twentieth century, inducing abortion was a crime in Sweden. The sale and dispensing of information about contraceptives was banned in 1910. The first law permitting abortion was passed in 1938. It remained in force with minor amendments until 1975. The 1938 act permitted abortion if the mother's life or health was seriously threatened, if she was a victim of rape or incest, or if there was a history of hereditary disease. The current Abortion Act was adopted in 1975. It permits abortion on request up to eighteen weeks of pregnancy. It is provided free. After eighteen weeks, abortions are legal only if the National Board of Health and Welfare grant authorization on special grounds. There are no penalties for a woman who terminates her own pregnancy. Non-physicians who perform or attempt to perform abortions are subject to fine or imprisonment for a maximum of one year.

Since 1975, between 30 and 37,000 abortions are performed annually, constituting a rate of 18.0 to 21.0 abortions per 1000 women aged 15 to 44 years of age.

United Kingdom

According to English Common Law, it was not considered murder to kill a child in the womb. It was a misdemeanor to do so after quickening. In 1861, the Offense Against the Person Act decreed that it was a criminal offense, punishable by life imprisonment, if the woman or any other person sought to procure a miscarriage. The Infant Life Preservation Act of 1929 made it a crime to kill a viable fetus (twenty-eight weeks or more) unless the death of the child was necessary to save the mother's life. In 1938, in the decision handed down in *Rex v. Bourne*, the grounds for abortion were extended to preserving the mother's mental or physical health.

The Abortion Law currently in effect in England, Scotland, and Wales is regulated by the Abortion Act of 1967, as amended by the Human Fertilization and Embryology Act of 1990. Both acts stipulate that abortion is legal within twenty-four weeks of gestation and must be obtained in a National Health Service hospital after two registered medical practitioners certify that the grounds have been met.

In July 1991, the United Kingdom became the second country, after France, to approve use of the abortion pill RU486. From 1970 to 1991, from 8.6 to 14.4 abortions were performed on 1000 women from the ages of 15 to 44. Most were done on single women aged 20 to 24.

Ireland

The Irish Constitution prohibits the voluntary termination of pregnancy. A 1983 referendum inserted even stronger language into the constitution and guaranteed that the government would defend the life of the unborn. A woman who seeks to procure an abortion may be imprisoned for life.

In February 1992, a 14-year-old Irish rape victim was prevented by the High Court from traveling to England to obtain an abortion. The Supreme Court overturned the High Court's decision and ruled that the life of the girl was endangered by a situation of emotional distress that could lead her to commit suicide. This interpretation is currently the law in Ireland. A national referendum held in November 1992 gained the right to travel abroad to obtain an abortion and to obtain information in Ireland about abortion services available abroad. Since 1992 between 4500 and 9000 Irish women have traveled to Britain each year for abortions.

In 1990, the abortion rate in Ireland was 5.4 per 1000 women aged 15 to 44.

Italy

Prior to 1975, abortion was permitted only if the mother's life was in danger. In 1975, the criteria was expanded to preserving the mother's life. As of 1978, and the passage of law No. 194, abortions are legal during the first ninety days of pregnancy to preserve the mother's health, if the child is likely to be born with a handicap, if the mother was the victim of rape or incest, or if the mother claims that her economic, social, or family situation is such that she cannot bear the child. After the first trimester, an abortion is allowed to save a woman's life or when the mother's physical or mental health is endangered. A one-week reflection period is imposed unless a physician and the mother sign a certificate claiming that an emergency situation exists. Abortions must be performed in a hospital. They are free of charge.

After the 1978 law was passed, the Holy See issued a warning that any person performing an abortion and any woman obtaining an abortion would be excommunicated. It is estimated that nearly 70 percent of physicians and a majority of other health care professionals have invoked the "conscience clause," which states that medical personnel opposed to abortion on moral or religious grounds can declare in advance their conscientious objections and be exempted from performing or assisting in the performance of an abortion.

As of 1990, the rate of abortion was 12.7 per 1000 women between 15 and 44 years of age.

Spain

Current criteria by which abortions may occur in Spain were enacted in July 1985. Organic Law No. 9 states abortions may be performed to avert a serious risk to the physical health or mental health of the pregnant woman; if the pregnancy was the result of rape, provided that the rape had been reported to the police and the abortion was performed within the first twelve weeks of pregnancy; or if the fetus, carried to term, would suffer from severe physical or mental defects, provided that the abortion was performed within the first twenty-two weeks of pregnancy. Prior to the 1985 legislation, abortions were permitted only to save the life of the pregnant woman.

By Order of the Ministry of Health, as of June 1986, all abortions must be reported to the national health authorities. An abortion that is performed because of fetal impairment must be certified by two specialists from an approved health center.

In January 1991, the Supreme Court sanctioned abortion for the first time on social grounds. The court dismissed a criminal case brought against a married couple and the friend who helped them, concluding that if the woman had been forced to give birth, her right to the development of her person would have been violated. This decision does not mean that the abortion law in Spain has been changed, especially since the court upheld the conviction of the physician involved. It indicates that in some cases, if a court so chooses, it may exonerate a pregnant woman from guilt on the basis of social grounds. A draft Penal Code published in February 1992 permits abortions to be performed on socio-economic grounds. In July 1994, a bill that would permit abortion on request after a compulsory three-day waiting period was submitted to the Parliament. Such abortions would have to be performed in private clinics.

From 1987 to 1991, the rate of abortions in Spain per 1000 women from 15 to 44 years of age was 2.0 to 4.8.

Summary

As shown by the preceding discussion, there is a broad range of criteria under which abortions may be obtained in Western Europe. Ireland prohibits abortions, and France permits abortions before the end of the tenth week. Spain permits abortions during the first trimester to preserve the physical and mental health of the mother if she is the victim of rape or incest, or if the fetus is impaired. Italy permits abortions for those reasons and for social, economic, and personal reasons.

Sweden, Denmark, the Netherlands, Austria, and Great Britain permit abortions on demand before the end of the first trimester. Germany permits abortions for medical and ethical reasons or for economic, social, and personal reasons only after a woman has agreed to undergo social counseling with a physician.

As border controls in Western Europe have become more and more relaxed, the number of women who cross them for the purpose of securing an abortion increases. Each year of the 1990s more than 15,000 European women crossed national borders in order to obtain an abortion. Irish, Italian, and French women have been going to Great Britain for abortions; German, French and Belgian women are traveling to the Netherlands; and women who live in southern France are crossing the border to Spain to obtain an abortion.

EASTERN EUROPE

Since the fall of communism there have been major changes in the abortion statutes in all of the countries that formed the Soviet-dominated Eastern European bloc. In the following section, we review statutes in a sample of those countries.

Belarus

Formerly one of the republics in the former Soviet Union, Belarus permits abortion on demand. The abortion must be performed by a licensed physician in a hospital with the consent of the woman.

The latest year for which data are available on abortion rates in Belarus was 1985, when it was reported 80 abortions per 1000 women between 15 and 49 years of age.

Bulgaria

Abortions are available on request if the woman is not more than twelve weeks pregnant. She may obtain an abortion if she is within twenty weeks of her pregnancy if a medical committee composed of the head of an obstetrics department and two physicians certifies that the pregnancy poses a threat to her life or health, or if the fetus is severely impaired. All abortions must be performed in authorized obstetrics hospitals by certified obstetricians.

Czech Republic and Slovenia

Up through the first twenty-six weeks, the consent of the woman and the authorization of her gynecologist are the only criteria for abortion in the new Czech Republic and in Slovenia. As recently as 1950 abortions were permitted only to save the mother's life or preserve her health. From 1957 to 1983 abortion laws were repeatedly amended all in the direction of greater liberalization. Prior to the mid 1980s, abortion was the preferred method of birth control. It was free, contraceptives were not, and in addition the latter were difficult to obtain.

The 1986 law provides contraceptives (not condoms) free of charge, but fees are charged for abortions performed after the eighth week. The abortion rates have increased drastically from 2.7 per 1000 women aged 15 to 44 in 1957 to 48.7 per 1000 women aged 15 to 44 in 1988.

Hungary

Under the most recent abortion statute adopted in December 1992, a woman can obtain a abortion up to the first twelve weeks of her pregnancy if she states that the pregnancy has caused a serious crisis for her. After the first trimester an abortion is legal if certain criteria are met: there is a misdiagnosis of the pregnancy, the woman is under 18 years of age, or there is genetic risk. The new law also includes a compulsory consultation with a nurse, who must inform the pregnant woman of the conditions and effects of abortion as well as the possibilities for assistance should she choose to carry the pregnancy to term. Abortions for medical reasons are free of charge.

Prior to 1952, abortion was illegal in Hungary. But from 1953 to 1973, laws were changed such that pregnancies could be terminated within the first twelve weeks on the woman's request. Then, from 1973 up to the passage of the 1992 statute currently in effect, restrictions were introduced. For example, following a decree in 1973, although abortion remained legal on social grounds, the following conditions were added: the woman had to be unmarried or separated, have inadequate housing, be 40 years or older, have a husband who was a regular solider, or she or her husband be in prison.

The rates of abortion in Hungary ranged from a high of 83.8 per 1000 women 15 to 44 years of age in 1970 to 35.6 in 1980. In 1990, the rate was 40.0 per 1000 women 15 to 44 years of age.

Poland

In May 1997, by a nine-three ruling, the Constitutional Tribunal passed legislation that would make abortion illegal in Poland (*L.A. Times*, May 27, 1997, p. A26). In adopting the new legislation President Andrzej Zoll stated, "The highest value in a democracy is human life which must be protected from its start to the end."

Until 1932, abortions were prohibited in Poland. From 1956 through 1993, laws were amended to allow and liberalize the criteria for abortion. Under legislation passed in February 1993, abortion was permitted when the life or health of the mother was threatened, there was a serious and irreversible malformation of the fetus, or the pregnancy was the result of rape or incest. The abortion had to be performed within the first twelve weeks of the pregnancy, and in a hospital. Even if the abortion was self-induced, the law did not provide for punishment for the woman, although physicians may face up to two years of imprisonment. The new 1997 ruling still permits abortion in cases of rape or incest or if the fetus was grossly deformed.

Abortion rates ranged from a high of 24.3 per 1000 women aged 15 to 44 in 1965 to a low of 3.6 in 1991.

Romania

Romania has one of the highest rates of abortion in the world. After dropping from 251.7 per 1000 women 15 to 44 years old in 1965 to 39.1 in 1989, it rose to 199.3 in 1990. In 1991, the abortion rate was 172.4 per 1000 women 15 to 44 years old.

Abortion was first legalized in 1957. Current law, passed in January 1990, allows abortion on request and removed restrictions on the sale and importation of contraceptives. In the mid 1980s, Romania introduced a campaign to increase the birth rate and to restrict abortions. For example, a decree passed in December 1985 stated that to qualify for an abortion, a woman must have given birth to a minimum of five children that were currently under her care. Married women who did not conceive were kept under surveillance and a special tax was levied on unmarried persons over 25 years of age as well as on childless couples that did not have a medical reason for not bearing children.

Russian Federation

In November 1920, abortion was legalized in the newly formed Union of Soviet Socialist Republics. It was the first experience in the world with the legalization of abortions on request and they were conducted free of charge in government hospitals. Abortions were illegal in Czarist Russia. In 1649, they were punishable by death. In the Russian Penal Code of 1895, both the pregnant woman and the abortion provider could be imprisoned for four to six years for performing an abortion.

After the formation of the Soviet Union and the legalization of abortion under Lenin's leadership in 1920, changes and restrictions began to be introduced beginning in 1924. For example, a 1924 statute introduced a fee for the performing of an abortion. A 1935 statute forbade termination of first pregnancies except for medical reasons. In 1936, the ban was extended to forbid abortions performed only for eugenic reasons. Some twenty years later in 1955, the government repealed the prohibition on abortion, and in regulations passed in 1956 and again in 1982 specified that abortions could be performed in the first trimester, but not if the pregnancy occurred within six months after a woman's previous abortion. The maximum penalty for an illegal abortion was eight years in a labor camp.

Order Number 1342, passed in December 1987, permits abortions during the first twenty-eight weeks on judicial, genetic, or broad medical and social grounds. Like Romania, the Russian Federation has a high rate of abortions. In 1970 it was 156.5 per 1000 women aged 15 to 44. In 1990 it was 119.6 and in 1991 it was 109.2. Russian health officials report that a typical Russian woman will have three to five abortions in her lifetime (CNN, September 1996). The high increase is attributable to a shortage of high quality contraceptives and lack of knowledge about them.

Summary

Even after the breakup of the Soviet-dominated Eastern bloc, the countries of Eastern Europe are more homogeneous in their laws and policies vis-à-vis abortion statutes than are the countries of Western Europe. With the exception of Poland, they permit abortions for a broad range of health, eugenic, and socioeconomic reasons.

ASIA

In shifting next to an examination of major Asian societies, we continue to find societies with statutes that permit abortions on demand or for a wide range of reasons.

China

With its policy of "one child per family," the Chinese government endorses the use of abortion as a means of population and birth control and permits it on request. The government also provides abortion services free of charge and allows the woman fourteen days paid sick leave if the pregnancy is terminated after the first trimester. Abortions are performed on request within six months of gestation. Up until the last years of the Qing dynasty, from 1644 to 1911, there were no laws regulating abortion. In the last period of the Qing dynasty and during the Republican era (1911–1949), abortions were declared illegal and punishable by fines, and/or imprisonment. The Mao regime, in its early period from 1950 to 1953, was pro-natalist and continued to make abortion illegal. But in 1953, it reversed its position. In 1979, China introduced the one child policy. In 1983, a nationwide campaign was conducted that included mandatory sterilization for couples with two or more children, abortion for unplanned pregnancies, and IUD (intrauterine device) insertions for women with one child. China is the only country in the world that assesses no penalty for having or performing an abortion at any stage of pregnancy, as long as the procedure is carried out by an authorized person. Abortion rates ranged from 23.1 in 1971 for 1000 women 15 to 44 years of age to a high of 61.5 in 1983, to 38.8 in 1987.

India

Although India does not impose the same restrictions on family size as China, since 1972 it also permits abortion on request during the first twenty weeks of gestation. Abortions are performed free of charge in government hospitals. The most recent data on abortion rates have them at 3.3 per 1000 women 15 to 44 years of age, as of 1989. Reports also indicate that 20 percent of maternal deaths are due to unsafe abortions.

India was the first country to introduce a family planning program in 1951. The major objective of the program was to control population growth. During the first and second five-year plans (1951–1961), the program's major activities involved providing information and advice to couples on the rhythm method, foam tablets, diaphragms, and jellies when they came to the family planning clinics.

By the mid-sixties, there was a clear shift to population control and the reduction of the birthrate within a stipulated period of time. Under Indira Gandhi's government in the 1970s, Emergency Powers were introduced and civil rights were suspended. In 1973–1974, 900,000 sterilizations were conducted; in 1974–1975, the numbers increased to 1.35 million; and in 1975–1976, to 2.5 million. The forced sterilization program was one of the major factors in the collapse of Indira Gandhi's government in 1977.

In the early 1980s, as procedures for determining the sex of the fetus became widely available, the abortion of female fetuses became common practice. A report released in 1989 claimed that from 1978 to 1982, 78,000 fetuses were aborted after sex determination tests (Patel, V. 1987). Another report based on a survey in Bombay stated that out of 8,000 abortions conducted after sex determination tests, 7999 involved female fetuses (*Statesman*, Dec. 17, 1984). In the late 1980s, states began passing laws that monitored and restricted the use of these tests.

Japan

As of 1949, abortions were made legal within the first twenty-four weeks for medical and for social and economic reasons. But impairment of the fetus was not considered a legitimate criterion. Before 1948, abortion had been considered a criminal act under a code derived from the French legal system and adopted in 1880.

A woman who performs an abortion on herself by the use of drugs or otherwise may be imprisoned for up to one year. A doctor, midwife, pharmacist, or druggist who at the request of a woman or with her consent causes her abortion may be imprisoned from three months to five years.

Abortion rates ranged from a high of 52.2 per 1000 women 15 to 44 years of age in 1955 to a low of 14.5 in 1990.

Republic of Korea

Prior to 1973, the Criminal Code of the Republic of Korea prohibited abortion on any grounds. In 1973, the Maternal and

Child Health Law permitted abortions on the following grounds: to save the mother's life, to preserve her physical and mental health, if she is a victim of rape or incest, or if there is fetal impairment. The consent of the woman as well as that of her spouse, if she is married, is required. Abortion may be performed within the first twenty-eight weeks of pregnancy.

Abortion rates have declined from 25.4 per 1000 married women aged 15 to 44 in 1983 to 6.4 in 1989.

Philippines

Unlike most of the non-Muslim countries of Asia, including the four cited above, abortion is illegal on any grounds in the Philippines. Its policies match closely those of Ireland. Its 1975 Child and Youth Welfare Code stipulated that a child has the dignity and worth of a human being from the moment of conception and has the right to be born well. Persons performing an abortion, with the woman's consent, are subject to imprisonment for six months to six years and a woman performing an abortion on herself is subject to the minimum or medium of that penalty. But, in 1990, the government instituted a new family planning program that established more incentives including tax exemptions for couples to limit the size of their families to two children.

Summary

In the major Asian countries, with the exception of the Philippines, statutes provide broad grounds for abortion into the second trimester and provide them free of charge in government hospitals.

OCEANIA

Australia

Although restrictions vary by state, in all regions abortions are available for reasons of the mother's physical and mental health, if she was the victim of rape or incest, or if the fetus is impaired. There are variations on personal, social, and economic grounds. The woman's consent is required in all states and none require the spouse's consent. Government health insurance benefits are available to all citizens for legal abortions.

From 1980 to 1988, the abortion rate per 1000 women aged 15 to 44 ranged from 13.9 to 16.6.

MIDDLE EAST AND NORTH AFRICA

Moving from Australia back across the Asian mainland, we report policies and practices in Muslim countries of the Middle East and North Africa. Although Islamic law generally forbids abortion, there are some variations between the Sunni and Shite Muslim societies and even within each of the different branches of Islam. We look first at the most traditional Sunni Islamic society.

Saudi Arabia

As of June 1989 and the passage of Ministerial Resolution Number 288/17 an abortion may be performed to save a woman's life and "if the pregnancy is less than four months old and it is proven beyond doubt that the continued pregnancy gravely endangers the mother's health." Written consent must be obtained from the woman as well as her husband or guardian and three medical specialists appointed by the hospital must sign a recommendation form before the abortion can be performed.

Egypt

The criteria in Egypt are comparable to those in Saudi Arabia. Abortions are prohibited except to save the mother's life. Her husband's consent is required and a committee of physicians must certify that the pregnancy poses a serious risk to the woman's life. Egyptian courts have ruled that the fetus is created at conception.

Turkey

Two Sunni Muslim countries that grant abortions on request are Tunisia and Turkey. In Turkey, until 1983, abortion was permitted in order to save the woman's life or to preserve her physical or mental health, if the pregnancy was the result of rape or incest, or in the case of fetal impairment. Since 1983, in part because of the growing incidence of unsafe abortions resulting in the mothers' deaths, abortion during the first ten weeks of pregnancy has been available on request, so long as the woman obtains the approval of her spouse or guardian. After the first ten weeks, abortion is permitted only to save the life or preserve the health of the mother or if there is evidence of fetal impairment. From 1985 to 1991 the rates of abortion ranged from 3.3 to 2.8 per 1000 women from 15 to 44 years of age.

Tunisia

Section 214 of the Tunisian Penal Code amended in 1973 permits abortions on request within the first trimester. Abortions, like all medical services, are subsidized by the government and must be performed by a physician in a hospital. Tunisia was the first Muslim country to liberalize its abortion law. Prior to 1973 abortions were prohibited.

From 1975 to 1991, abortion rates per 1000 women aged 15 to 44 ranged from 13.7 to 10.8.

Iran

Iraq and Iran are the two major Shite Muslim countries in the Middle East. Iran permits abortion to save the life of the mother. From 1973 to 1979, Iran legalized abortion and permitted it for health reasons or if the mother was a victim of rape or incest. But after the overthrow of the Shah in 1979, abortion was declared illegal except to save the mother's life.

Iraq

Criteria for abortion are broader in Iraq than Iran. Iraq permits abortion to save the mother's life or to preserve her physical or mental health, if the woman was the victim of rape or incest, or if the fetus is impaired. The woman's husband must give his consent in writing and she must have the recommendation of two medical specialists. Violations may result in imprisonment for the woman of one year and a longer term for the physician involved.

Israel

Unlike the neighboring Arab and Islamic states, Israel permits abortions on the written request of women if they are approved by a committee of two physicians and a social worker. At the time of the establishment of the state in 1948, Israel adopted the British Act of 1861, which restricted the grounds on which an abortion could be obtained, and subjected a woman who induced her own abortion to serve years in prison. A person performing an illegal abortion could be imprisoned for fourteen years. In 1977, Israel passed a criminal law amendment that both extended the grounds on which abortions could be performed and abolished any penalties on a woman who induced her own abortion. The 1977 act also reduced the penalty imposed on a person who performed an induced abortion from fourteen to five years of imprisonment, or a fine.

Most abortions are performed on married women. In 1990, the rate was 14.9 per 1000 women aged 15 to 44. In 1997, the head of the obstetrics and gynecology department Professor Shlomo Mashiah at Sheba Hospital reported that there are about 16,000 abortions per year in Israel and that that figure has remained constant since 1989. There are also, he claimed, about 4000 to 6000 illegal abortions annually (*Jerusalem Post*, March 22, 1997, p. 4).

Summary

Our review thus far has taken us through Western and Eastern Europe, parts of Asia, Australia, and the Middle East. In the first four regions, abortions are generally permitted in the first trimester for a wide range of reasons or on demand. They are also generally subsidized by the government. In Western Europe, Ireland and the Holy See are the clear exceptions to this pattern. Their statutes forbidding abortion are comparable to the Muslim countries represented by Egypt and Saudi Arabia, and like them are based on religious prohibitions. We turn next to countries in Africa.

AFRICA

Most African countries with the exceptions of Tunisia, Ghana, and Liberia place strong restrictions on induced abortions.

Nigeria

An abortion may be induced only if the pregnancy poses a serious threat to the mother's life. Punishment for the woman who induces an abortion is seven years imprisonment, for a physician up to fourteen years imprisonment.

Ghana

As of 1985, abortion is legal in Ghana if the life or mental or physical health of the mother is at risk, if there is substantial risk that the child will be handicapped, or if the pregnancy is the result of rape or incest. The abortion must be performed in an approved hospital by a registered physician and with the consent of the pregnant woman.

Any person administering a poison or other noxious substance to a woman or using any instruments or other means to cause an abortion is guilty of an offense and is liable to imprisonment for a term not exceeding five years, regardless of whether the woman is pregnant or has given her consent.

Kenya

Kenya permits abortion only if the mother's life is in danger. It must be performed by a certified physician with the consent of the woman and her spouse. It must be performed in a hospital after two medical opinions have been obtained, one of which must be from the physician who is treating her and the other from a psychiatrist. Persons performing an illegal abortion may be imprisoned for up to thirteen years and women who induce their own abortion may be imprisoned for up to seven years.

Although official abortion statistics are not available, data obtained from hospitals in 1988 and 1989 showed that over half of all gynecological admissions were due to abortions.

Liberia

As of 1979, abortion is permitted if the mother's life is in danger, if her physical or mental health is threatened, if she was a victim of rape or incest or other felonious intercourse (i.e., intercourse when she is under 16 years of age), or if the fetus is impaired. Two physicians, one of whom may be the one performing the abortion, must certify in writing that the need for an abortion meet any of the criteria described above.

Although official data are not available, illegal abortions are particularly common among urban adolescent women. In 1986, a national health survey found that only 6 percent of women of reproductive age were using modern methods of contraception.

South Africa

As of 1975, an abortion may be obtained to preserve the physical or mental health of the mother, if she is a victim of rape or incest, or if the fetus is impaired. It must be performed in a government hospital after two independent physicians (not including the doctor who will perform the abortion) approve the action and the hospital superintendent grants his/her permission. The 1975 law also specifies that physicians and nurses who do not wish to assist with an abortion, on grounds of conscience, are not obliged to do so. Women who procure abortions in violation of the 1975 act face imprisonment for up to five years and/or a fine not exceeding 500 rand.

Prior to the passage of the 1975 act, abortion law was governed by Roman-Dutch common law, which permitted an abortion only if the life of the mother would be endangered by continuation of the pregnancy.

The abortion rate in 1987 was .1 per 1000 women aged 15 to 44.

Summary

The African nations cited above have criteria similar to Ireland and to Muslim countries in the Middle East.

SOUTH AMERICA

We are now ready to cross the Atlantic and Pacific oceans and examine abortion criteria in the Western Hemisphere. We begin with countries in South America in which abortion is granted usually to save the mother's life, in a few countries to preserve her health, or if she has been a victim of rape or incest.

Argentina

The criteria for abortion is the preservation of the mother's life and physical health. A person inducing an abortion may be punished by imprisonment for three to ten years if it is done without the woman's consent, and for fifteen years if the women dies. If it is done with the woman's consent, the punishment is one to four years imprisonment and six years if the woman dies. Women who induce their own abortion may be imprisoned for up to four years.

As of 1986, family planning was made legal and available in the private sector, but not easily available for women who, for economic reasons, must rely on the public sector. Outside the Eastern European countries, Argentina has among the highest abortion rates in the world. One abortion is estimated to occur for every two live births.

Brazil

Abortion may be induced to save the mother's life or if she was the victim of rape or incest. It must be performed by a physician. A woman who procures an abortion for another reason faces at least four years in prison. A physician also is punishable by at least four years imprisonment.

Chile

The Children's Civil Code protects life from the time of conception and does not permit abortion on any grounds. Anyone who performs an abortion with the woman's consent is subject to up to three years in prison. A woman who induces her own abortion is subject to three to five years in prison.

Venezuela

Under the 1964 Criminal Code, an abortion may be performed only to save the woman's life. It may be performed only with the written consent of the woman, her husband, or her legal representative. Punishment for the person who performs an illegal abortion is imprisonment for twelve to thirty months, for the woman it is six months to two years. Official data report that from 1980 through 1983, illegal abortions accounted for 24.6 percent of all maternal deaths.

CENTRAL AMERICA AND THE CARIBBEAN

The criteria for abortion in the Caribbean and Central American countries show somewhat greater variation than the very strict ones operating in Latin America.

Mexico

The Mexican Criminal Code of January 1931, which applies in the Federal District and throughout Mexico to all offenses that fall within the jurisdiction of the federal courts, declared abortion to be generally illegal except when it is performed to save the life of the mother or if the mother was the victim of rape or incest. Except for emergency cases, a legal abortion must be performed by a physician whose opinion concerning the necessity of the abortion is corroborated by another physician.

Any person performing an abortion with the consent of the woman is subject to imprisonment for from one to three years, without consent, from six to eight years. A woman inducing her own abortion may be imprisoned for from six months to five years.

Each state has its own abortion provisions in its criminal code, many of which are nearly identical to those of the Federal District. But in the 1980s some states passed more liberal provisions including the right to abortion for "serious and substantial economic reasons in cases where the woman has at least three children."

Estimates from studies conducted in the 1980s indicate that approximately 800,000 illegal abortions were induced each year and each year about 24 percent of the women of reproductive age were estimated to have undergone an abortion.

Belize

Of all the countries in Central America, Belize, as of December 1980, has the most liberal criteria for induced abortion. The grounds include: to preserve the mother's life or her physical or mental health, if she is a victim of rape or incest, if the fetus is impaired, or for specified social and economic reasons.

The punishments for illegal abortions are severe: fourteen years for anyone performing an illegal abortion, and for a woman who induces her own abortion, she is subject to life imprisonment.

Costa Rica

The Costa Rican Penal Code of May 1970 permits abortion only to save the life of the mother or to preserve her physical health. The abortion may be performed only after obtaining the written consent of the pregnant woman, her husband or a legal representative, and after prior consultation with two additional physicians. Illegal abortions are punishable by imprisonment for from one to three years. The same punishment is applied to a woman who induces her own abortion.

Honduras

The 1906 Penal Code declared abortion to be illegal on all grounds. But according to the Fundamental Law Decree Number 94, passed in June 1964, a physician may perform an abortion for therapeutic reasons. Written consent of the mother, her husband, or closest relative is required as is the written opinion of a medical committee.

Any person who performs an illegal abortion with the pregnant woman's consent is subject to imprisonment for from two to three years. A woman who induces her own abortion is subject to the same penalty.

Jamaica

The 1938 decision in *Rex v. Browne* in the United Kingdom has been applied in Jamaica since 1975. It permits abortion in order to preserve the physical and mental health of the mother. The spouse's consent plus the approval of two specialists are required to perform an abortion if the mother is the victim of rape or incest or the fetus is impaired. A person who procures or attempts to procure an illegal abortion is subject to life imprisonment or to imprisonment for not less than three years.

Cuba

Like the former communist countries of Eastern Europe, since 1965, Cuba permits abortion on request up through the tenth week of gestation through the National Health System. If the woman is unmarried and under 16 years of age, parental permission is required. The abortion must be performed by a physician in an official health center. Abortions may be obtained in the second trimester if they are authorized by a committee of obstetricians, psychologists, and social workers.

From 1968 to 1974, the rates of legal abortions quadrupled, increasing from 16.7 to 69.5 per 1000 women 15 to 44 years of age. From 1974 through 1984 they ranged between 69.5 and 47.2. Even though abortion has been legal since the late 1960s, induced abortion was the leading cause of maternal death among women aged 20 to 34 from 1979 to 1982.

Summary

In November 1994, the World Health Organization reported that countries in Latin American and the Caribbean "have the highest documented evidence of unsafe induced abortion among the regions of the developing world." It estimated that the yearly number of abortions in that region was between four and six million. Most of these abortions, the report continued, were performed using inadequate techniques under unhygienic conditions and without medical supervision. The statutes in most of the countries of Central America, including Mexico, permit abortion to save the mother's life or if she is the victim of rape or incest; in Costa Rica, to preserve her physical health; in Honduras, abortion is illegal on all grounds. In Belize, abortion is permitted on all of the above grounds, plus social and economic reasons. Among the countries in the Caribbean, Jamaica permits abortion on grounds of preserving the mother's physical and mental health, if the woman was the victim of rape or incest, or if the fetus is impaired. Cuba permits abortion on request. With the exception of Honduras, the countries of Central America and the Caribbean have more liberal abortion statutes than do the countries of South America in which abortion is either prohibited or permitted only if the mother's life is endangered.

Moving farther north, we come to the United States and Canada.

NORTH AMERICA

United States

As of 1973 and the U.S. Supreme Court decision in *Roe v. Wade*, abortions are permitted in all states prior to fetal viability (defined as occurring from 24 to 28 weeks of gestation). After fetal viability, a state may prohibit an abortion only if it provides exception for endangerment to the woman's life or health.

Abortions before quickening were permitted by traditional common law until 1845 when the first of many states passed laws prohibiting all abortions. By the early 1960s, forty-one states permitted abortion only if the life of the mother was threatened; the remaining states did so if the woman's life or physical health was in jeopardy. The 1973 Supreme Court decision ruled that a woman's decision to have an abortion in the first trimester should be exclusively between herself and her physician. The Court also held that a fetus was not a person and was therefore not entitled to protection guaranteed by the Constitution until it reached the point of viability. Since 1973, the Court's rulings in the 1980s and 1990s have cut back on some of the Constitutional grounds guaranteed in *Roe v. Wade*. For example, *Webster v. Reproductive Health Service*, 1989, barred the use of public-funded employees or buildings for abortions, and required abortion providers to conduct tests to determine whether a fetus that was believed to be at least twenty weeks old was viable.

In 1992, in its decision in *Planned Parenthood of Southeastern Pennsylvania v. Casey*, the Court reaffirmed that a woman has a constitutional right to obtain an abortion prior to fetal viability and that a state may prohibit an abortion thereafter only if it provides exceptions for endangerment to the woman's life or health. Although the *Casey* ruling left no doubt that laws prohibiting abortion were unconstitutional, the Court rejected the trimester framework set forth in *Roe* and held that states have legitimate interests in protecting the health of the woman and the life of the unborn child from the onset of pregnancy. In May 1997, the U.S. Senate approved legislation that would ban "partial-birth" abortion by a vote of sixty-four to thirty-six, but it fell three votes shy of the needed two-thirds margin to override a promised Presidential veto. Early in the year, the U.S. House of Representatives had passed the legislation by more than enough votes to override a veto. The bill seeks to ban a procedure under which a surgeon pulls the fetus out of the birth canal feet first and then punctures the head, removes the brain, and collapses the skull so the fetus can be removed vaginally. It could be used only to save a woman's life, not to protect her health. Of the estimated 1,529,000 abortions performed each year, 16,000 are performed after the twentieth week and are known as late-term abortions (Barbara Kantrowitz, "A Bitter New Battle over Partial Birth Abortions," *Newsweek*, March 17, 1997; based on a survey for the Alan Guttmacher Institute).

Abortion restrictions still vary by state; thirty-five have laws that prevent a minor from obtaining an abortion without parental consent or notice. Eleven states have mandatory waiting periods of at least twenty-four hours. In 1977, Congress barred the use of federal funds to pay for abortions, and as of 1992, thirteen states pay for abortions of low income women.

As of 1988, 83 percent of women who obtained abortions were unmarried, 84 percent were under 25 years old. Women who earned less than $15,000 per year were 1.6 to 2.2 times as likely to have an abortion and women who lived with a partner outside of marriage or who made no religious identification were 3.5 to 4.0 times as likely as women in the general population to have an abortion (Alan Guttmacher Institute). From 1975 through 1991, abortion rates per 1000 women 15 to 44 years old exhibited a fluctuating rise from 21.7 to 29.3. The year 1980 was the highpoint at 29.3. In 1991, the rate was 26.4.

Canada

As of January 1988, abortions have been available on demand and there are no stipulations as to who must perform them and where. Prior to 1969, abortion was legal only if the mother's life and health were endangered. The Canadian Supreme Court struck down the 1969 law on the grounds that it infringed on the principles of life, liberty, and security of persons contained in the Canadian Charter of Rights and Freedom.

Abortion rates have ranged from 6.6 per 1000 women aged 15 to 44 in 1971 to 11.6 in 1979. Between 1979 and 1987 they dropped to 10.2 per 1000 women of child bearing age.

Table 2.1
Abortion Policy Across the Globe, 1994

	To save the woman's life	To preserve physical health	To preserve mental health	Rape or Incest	Fetal impairment	Economic or social reasons	On request
AFRICA							
Eastern Africa							
Burundi	X	X	--	--	--	--	--
Comoros	X	X	--	--	--	--	--
Djibouti	--	--	--	--	--	--	--
Eritrea	X	X	--	--	--	--	--
Ethiopia	X	X	--	--	--	--	--
Kenya	X	--	--	--	--	--	--
Madagascar	X	--	--	--	--	--	--
Malawi	X	X	--	--	--	--	--
Mauritius	--	--	--	--	--	--	--
Mozambique	X	--	--	--	--	--	--
Rwanda	X	X	--	--	--	--	--
Seychelles	X	X	X	X	X	--	--
Somalia	X	--	--	--	--	--	--
Uganda	X	X	X	--	--	--	--
Tanzania	X	X	X	--	--	--	--

Zambia	X	X	X	--	--	--	--
Zimbabwe	X	X	--	X	X	--	--
Middle Africa							
Angola	X	--	--	--	--	--	--
Cameroon	X	X	--	X	--	--	--
Central African Republic	–	–	–	–	–	–	–
Chad	X	--	--	--	--	--	--
Congo	X	X	--	--	--	--	--
Equatorial Guinea	X	--	--	--	--	--	--
Gabon	X	--	--	--	--	--	--
SaoTome and Principe	--	--	--	--	--	--	--
Zaire	X	--	--	--	--	--	--
Northern Africa							
Algeria	X	X	X	X	--	--	--
Egypt	--	--	--	--	--	--	--
Libya	X	--	--	--	--	--	--
Morocco	X	X	--	--	--	--	--
Sudan	X	--	--	X	--	--	--
Tunisia	X	X	X	X	X	X	X

Table 2.1 (continued)

	To save the woman's life	To preserve physical health	To preserve mental health	Rape or incest	Fetal impairment	Economic or social reasons	On request
Southern Africa							
Botswana	X	X	X	X	X	--	--
Lesotho	X	--	--	--	--	--	--
Namibia	X	X	X	X	X	--	--
South Africa	X	X	X	X	X	--	--
Swaziland	X	X	X	--	--	--	--
Western Africa							
Benin	X	--	--	--	--	--	--
Burkina Faso	X	X	--	--	--	--	--
Cape Verde	X	X	X	X	X	X	--
Ivory Coast	X	--	--	--	--	--	--
Gambia	X	X	X	--	--	--	--
Ghana	X	X	X	X	X	--	--
Guinea	X	--	--	--	--	--	--
Guinea-Bissau	X	--	--	--	--	--	--
Liberia	X	X	X	X	X	--	--
Mali	X	--	--	--	--	--	--
Mauritania	X	--	--	--	--	--	--

Niger	X	--	--	--	--	--	--
Nigeria	X	--	--	--	--	--	--
Senegal	X	--	--	--	--	--	--
Sierra Leone	X	X	X	--	--	--	--
Togo	X	--	--	--	--	--	--
ASIA							
Eastern Asia							
China	X	X	X	X	X	X	X
Democratic People's Republic of Korea	X	X	X	X	X	X	X
Japan	X	X	X	X	--	X	--
Mongolia	X	X	X	X	X	X	X
Republic of Korea	X	X	X	X	X	--	--
South Eastern Asia							
Brunei	X	--	--	--	--	--	--
Cambodia	X	--	--	--	--	--	--
Indonesia	X	--	--	--	--	--	--
Lao People's Democratic Republic	X	--	--	--	--	--	--

Table 2.1 (continued)

	To save the woman's life	To preserve physical health	To preserve mental health	Rape or incest	Fetal impairment	Economic or social reasons	On request
Malaysia	X	X	X	--	X	--	--
Myanmar	X	--	--	--	--	--	--
Philippines	--	--	--	--	--	--	--
Singapore	X	X	X	X	X	X	X
Thailand	X	X	--	X	X	--	--
Vietnam	X	X	X	X	X	X	X
South Central Asia							
Afghanistan	X	--	--	--	--	--	--
Bangladesh	X	--	--	--	--	--	--
Bhutan	--	--	--	--	--	--	--
India	X	X	X	X	X	--	--
Iran	X	--	--	--	--	--	--
Kazakhstan	X	X	X	X	X	X	X
Kyrgyzstan	X	X	X	X	X	X	X
Maldives	X	X	--	--	--	--	--
Nepal	--	--	--	--	--	--	--
Pakistan	X	X	X	--	--	--	--

Sri Lanka	X	--	--	--	--	--	--
Tajikistan	X	X	X	X	X	X	X
Turkmenistan	X	X	X	X	X	X	X
Uzbekistan	X	X	X	X	X	X	X
Western Asia							
Armenia	X	X	X	X	X	X	X
Azerbaijan	X	X	X	X	X	X	X
Bahrain	X	X	X	--	X	--	--
Cyprus	X	X	X	X	X	--	--
Georgia	X	X	X	X	X	X	X
Iraq	X	X	X	X	X	--	--
Israel	X	X	X	X	X	--	--
Jordan	X	X	X	--	--	--	--
Kuwait	X	X	X	--	X	--	--
Lebanon	X	--	--	--	--	--	--
Oman	X	--	--	--	--	--	--
Qatar	X	X	--	--	X	--	--
Saudi Arabia	X	X	--	--	X	--	--
Syrian Arab Republic	X	--	--	--	--	--	--
Turkey	X	X	X	X	X	X	X

Table 2.1 (continued)

	To save the woman's life	To preserve physical health	To preserve mental health	Rape or incest	Fetal impairment	Economic or social reasons	On request
United Arab Emirates	X	--	--	--	--	--	--
Yemen	X	--	--	--	--	--	--
EUROPE							
Eastern Europe							
Belarus	X	X	X	X	X	X	X
Bulgaria	X	X	X	X	X	X	X
Czech Republic	X	X	X	X	X	X	X
Hungary	X	X	X	X	X	X	--
Poland	X	X	--	X	X	--	--
Republic of Moldova	X	X	X	X	X	X	X
Romania	X	X	X	X	X	X	X
Russian Federation	X	X	X	X	X	X	X
Slovakia	X	X	X	X	X	X	X
Ukraine	X	X	X	X	X	X	X
Northern Europe							
Denmark	X	X	X	X	X	X	X

Estonia	X	X	X	X	X	X	X
Finland	X	X	X	X	X	X	--
Iceland	X	X	X	X	X	X	--
Ireland	X	--	--	--	--	--	--
Latvia	X	X	X	X	X	X	X
Lithuania	X	X	X	X	X	X	X
Norway	X	X	X	X	X	X	X
Sweden	X	X	X	X	X	X	X
United Kingdom	X	X	X	--	X	X	--
Southern Europe							
Albania	X	X	X	X	X	X	X
Andorra	--	--	--	--	--	--	--
Bosnia and Herzegovina	X	X	X	X	X	X	X
Croatia	X	X	X	X	X	X	X
Greece	X	X	X	X	X	X	X
Holy See	--	--	--	--	--	--	--
Italy	X	X	X	X	X	X	--
Malta	--	--	--	--	--	--	--
Portugal	X	X	X	X	X	--	--
San Marino	--	--	--	--	--	--	--

Table 2.1 (continued)

	To save the woman's life	To preserve physical health	To preserve mental health	Rape or incest	Fetal impairment	Economic or social reasons	On request
Slovenia	X	X	X	X	X	X	X
Spain	X	X	X	X	X	--	--
Macedonia	X	X	X	X	X	X	X
Yugoslavia	X	X	X	X	X	X	X
Western Europe							
Austria	X	X	X	X	X	X	X
Belgium	X	X	X	X	X	X	--
France	X	X	X	X	X	X	--
Germany	X	X	X	X	X	--	--
Liechtenstein	X	X	X	--	--	--	--
Luxembourg	X	X	X	X	X	X	--
Monaco	X	--	--	--	--	--	--
Netherlands	X	X	X	X	X	X	X
Switzerland	X	X	X	--	--	--	--
LATIN AMERICA AND THE CARIBBEAN							
Caribbean							

Antigua and Barbuda	X	--	--	--	--	--	--
Bahamas	X	X	X	--	--	--	--
Barbados	X	X	X	X	X	X	--
Cuba	X	X	X	X	X	X	X
Dominica	X	--	--	--	--	--	--
Dominican Republic	--	--	--	--	--	--	--
Grenada	X	X	X	--	--	--	--
Haiti	X	--	--	--	--	--	--
Jamaica	X	X	X	--	--	--	--
St. Kitts and Nevis	X	X	X	--	--	--	--
St. Lucia	X	X	X	--	--	--	--
St. Vincent and the Gren	X	X	X	X	X	--	--
Trinidad and Tobago	X	X	X	--	--	--	--
Central America							
Belize	X	X	X	X	X	X	--
Costa Rica	X	X	--	--	--	--	--
El Salvador	X	--	--	X	X	--	--

Table 2.1 (continued)

	To save the woman's life	To preserve physical health	To preserve mental health	Rape or incest	Fetal impairment	Economic or social reasons	On request
Guatemala	X	--	--	--	--	--	--
Honduras	--	--	--	--	--	--	--
Mexico	X	--	--	X	--	--	--
Nicaragua	X	--	--	--	--	--	--
Panama	X	--	--	X	X	--	--
South America							
Argentina	X	X	--	--	--	--	--
Bolivia	X	X	--	X	--	--	--
Brazil	X	--	--	X	--	--	--
Chile	--	--	--	--	--	--	--
Colombia	--	--	--	--	--	--	--
Ecuador	X	X	--	X	--	--	--
Guyana	X	X	X	--	--	--	--
Paraguay	X	X	--	--	--	--	--
Peru	X	X	--	--	--	--	--
Suriname	X	--	--	--	--	--	--
Uruguay	X	X	--	--	--	--	--

Venezuela	X	--	--	--	--	--	--
Northern America							
Canada	X	X	X	X	X	X	X
United States	X	X	X	X	X	X	X
OCEANIA							
Australia	X	X	X	X	X	X	--
New Zealand	X	X	X	X	X	--	--
Melanesia							
Fiji	X	X	X	--	--	--	--
New Guinea	X	X	X	--	--	--	--
Solomon Islands	X	--	--	--	--	--	--
Vanuata	X	X	--	--	--	--	--
Micronesia							
Kiribati	X	--	--	--	--	--	--
Marshall Islands	X	X	X	--	--	--	--
Nauru	X	--	--	--	--	--	--
Polynesia							
Samoa	X	X	X	--	--	--	--
Tonga	X	--	--	--	--	--	--

Table 2.1 (continued)

Tuvalu	X	--	--	--	--	--	--
Permitted	173	119	94	81	79	54	41
Not permitted	16	70	95	108	110	135	148
Total Countries	189	189	189	189	189	189	189

Note: X = abortion permitted; — = abortion prohibited.

Summary

The United States and Canada, unlike its neighbors to the south, permit abortion on demand. They are closer to the largely Protestant countries of Western Europe than to the other nations in the Western Hemisphere.

ADDITIONAL DATA ACROSS THE GLOBE

The information in Table 2.1 was obtained from the United Nations Department of Economics and Social Information and Policy Analysis. It describes abortion policy as of 1994 for 189 nations.

Of the 189 countries, all but sixteen permit abortions if the mother's life is at stake. The countries that do not are: Djibouti, Mauritius, Central African Republic, São Tomé and Príncipe, and Egypt in Africa; the Philippines, Bhutan, and Nepal in Asia; Andorra, the Holy See, Malta, and San Marino in Europe; and the Dominican Republic, Honduras, Chile, and Columbia in the Caribbean and Central and South America. Those countries do not permit abortions on any grounds.

An additional 54 countries do not permit abortions to preserve the physical health of the mother. Twenty-one of those countries are in Africa, 14 in Asia, two in Europe, 12 in the Caribbean and Central and South America, and 5 in the Pacific Isles.

An additional twenty-four nations do not permit abortions to preserve the mother's mental health. They include 11 African countries, 4 Asian, 1 European, 7 Central and South American, and 1 in the Pacific Isles.

Twenty-four nations that permit abortion to save the mother's life or to preserve her physical or mental health do not permit them if the mother was the victim of rape or incest. Six of those countries are in Africa, 5 in Asia, 3 in Europe, 7 in the Caribbean and Central and South America, and 4 in the Pacific Isles. The Sudan, Cameroon, Zimbabwe, Thailand, Poland, El Salvador, Mexico, Panama, Brazil, and Ecuador permit abortions on the grounds of rape or incest, but not to preserve the mother's physical or mental health.

Two countries, Algeria and Japan, that permit abortions on all four of the above mentioned criteria do not permit them if the fetus is believed to be impaired. The United Kingdom permits abortions if the fetus is impaired, but not if the mother is the victim of rape or incest.

Less than one third of the 189 nations permit abortions for economic or social reasons. All of them except Japan also permit abortions for the five criteria (mother's life, physical health, mental health, mother is the victim of rape or incest, and fetal impairment) cited earlier. Finally, of the 189 nations, 41 permit abortions on request. Tunisia is the only African country to do so. In Eastern Asia, China, North Korea, Mongolia, Singapore, and Vietnam do so. Countries in Western Asia that separated from the former Soviet Union, plus Turkey, also permit them. In Eastern and Northern Europe nations that split off from the Soviet bloc, save Hungary and Poland, permit them. Denmark, Austria, the Netherlands, Norway, Sweden, and Greece are the other European nations that permit abortions on demand. Across the Atlantic, only Cuba, Canada, and the United States permit abortions on demand.

According to Dr. Yvette Delph of the World Health Organization, about two hundred million pregnancies occur worldwide of which twenty million are aborted in unsafe conditions, resulting in 70,000 maternal deaths (Technical Report 31, UN Population Fund, December 9, 1994). Unsafe abortion is one of the leading causes of the more than 500,000 maternal deaths that occur each year in the world, claims Carla Abou-Zaki of the World Health Organization (WHO) Maternal Health and Safe Motherhood Programme. She states further, "In some Latin American countries as many as half of all maternal deaths are abortion related" (Press release WHO, November 15, 1994).

Tables 2.2, 2.3, and 2.4 describe countries that have the highest and lowest abortion rates. Unfortunately, none of the countries in Africa report rates of abortion.

All of the countries listed in Table 2.2 permit abortions on

Table 2.2
Countries with the Highest Abortion Rates, 1988–1991

Country	Rate*	Year**
Romania	172.4	1991
Russia	119.6	1990
Belarus	114.3	1990
Ukraine	93.3	1990
Yugoslavia	91.4	1988
Kazakhstan	85.4	1990
Vietnam	83.5	1990
Moldavia	82.7	1990
Bulgaria	77.0	1990
Kyrgyzstan	76.3	1990
Latvia	70.0	1990

Table 2.3
Additional Countries That Permit Abortion on Demand, 1987–1991

Country	Rate	Year
China	37.5	1989
Mongolia	44.0	1991
Czech Republic	15.0	1991
Finland	11.0	1990
Norway	16.7	1991
Sweden	20.4	1990
Denmark	18.3	1987
Canada	11.2	1990
USA	26.4	1991

Table 2.4
Countries with the Lowest Abortion Rates, 1988–1991

Country	Rate	Year
Turkey	2.8	1991
India	3.2	1990
Bangladesh	3.2	1990
Poland	3.6	1991
Greece	3.6	1989
Spain	4.8	1991
Belgium	5.1	1991
Netherlands	5.2	1991
Ireland	5.4	1990
Korea	6.4	1989
Malaysia	6.4	1988

demand. The rates of abortions per year for the other countries that permit abortions on demand and for which abortion rates are available are shown in Table 2.3.

The countries of the former Soviet bloc plus Yugoslavia and Vietnam permit abortions on demand and have the highest rates. The other "on demand" abortion countries have rates that vary from 44.0 to 11.0 per year.

Table 2.4 lists the countries with the lowest abortion rates.

Included in this list are Bangladesh and Ireland in which the only grounds for abortion is to save the mother's life; and Turkey, Greece, and the Netherlands which permit abortions on demand. Poland, Greece, Spain, and Belgium, the other European countries on the list, are primarily Catholic countries. No other country that does not permit abortion except to save the mother's life reports abortion rates.

NOTE

1. *Abortion Policies: A Global Review* (New York: United Nations, 1995) provided much of the source materials for this chapter.

3

Public Opinion about Abortion

From 1981 through 1984, and then again from 1990 through 1994, Gallup Organizations all over the world joined with survey research centers in selective countries to coordinate an international survey of public attitudes about the conditions (if any) under which abortions should be permitted. Twenty-one nations participated in the 1981–1984 survey and forty participated in the 1991–1994 survey. All of the countries except Australia that participated in the 1981–1984 survey also participated in the 1991–1994 survey. The additional nineteen countries that participated only in the second survey were mostly from Eastern Europe and Asia.[1] The total number of respondents involved during both time periods was 89,908: 30,739 in the first and 59,169 in the second. The same questions were asked in both surveys. They were:

Do you approve or disapprove of abortion under the following circumstances:

1. When the mother's health is at risk by the pregnancy?

Table 3.1
Public Opinion, 1981–1984, 1991–1994

Approve/disapprove of abortion when the mother's health is at risk

Response	Percent
Approve	81.6
Disapprove	11.4
No answer	6.4
Don't know	0.6

Approve/disapprove of abortion when it is likely that the child will be born with a physical handicap

Response	Percent
Approve	68.4
Disapprove	23.6
No answer	6.4
Don't know	1.6

Approve/disapprove of abortion when the mother is not married

Response	Percent
Approve	30.5
Disapprove	60.3
No answer	6.8
Don't know	2.3

Approve/disapprove of abortion when the married couple does not want to have more children

Response	Percent
Approve	36.3
Disapprove	55.2
No answer	6.4
Don't know	2.1

Table 3.2
Public Opinion by Gender, 1981–1984, 1991–1994

Approve/disapprove when the mother's health is at risk

Response	Men	Women
Approve	88.4	87.6
Disapprove	11.6	12.4
Total N	37996	41229

Approve/disapprove when it is likely the child will be born with a physical handicap

Response	Men	Women
Approve	73.5	75.0
Disapprove	26.5	25.0
Total N	37586	40746

Approve/disapprove when the woman is not married

Response	Men	Women
Approve	34.1	32.8
Disapprove	65.9	57.2
Total N	36957	40325

Approve/disapprove when the married couple does not want to have more children

Response	Men	Women
Approve	40.9	38.6
Disapprove	59.1	61.4
Total N	37352	40513

Table 3.3
Public Opinion by Age, 1981–1984, 1991–1994

	18-24	25-34	35-44	45-54	55-64	65 and older
Mother's Health						
Approve	88.4	90.3	88.5	85.5	85.2	82.0
Disapprove	12.6	10.7	11.5	14.5	14.8	18.0
Total N	15,552	17,742	15,563	11,859	10,254	8,255
Child-Handicapped						
Approve	71.7	76.0	76.7	72.2	73.4	67.8
Disappove	28.3	24.0	23.3	27.8	26.6	32.2
Total N	15,316	17,583	15,464	11,769	10,122	8,128
Woman not married						
Approve	31.6	31.3	29.1	26.5	23.6	23.3
Disapprove	66.7	68.7	70.9	73.5	76.4	26.7
Total N	15,255	17,341	15,209	11,596	10.074	7,992
Couple doesn't want more children						
Approve	33.4	36.7	35.5	30.9	29.2	25.0
Disapprove	66.6	63.3	64.5	69.1	70.8	75.0
Total N	15,330	17,481	15,340	11,691	10,130	7,983

2. When it is likely that the child would be born physically handicapped?
3. When the mother is not married?
4. When a married couple does not want to have any more children?

Having examined the responses within each of the two time periods and found them to be similar, the data shown in Table 3.1 report the aggregate responses on both surveys for all of the nations involved. The answers show a clear preference. Most respondents support or approve of a woman seeking an abortion if her health is threatened or if it is likely that the baby will be physically handicapped. On the other hand, although with not quite as strong a majority preference, most respondents disapprove of a woman seeking an abortion because she is not married, or of a married couple wanting the wife to obtain an abortion because they do not want to have more children.

Before turning to an explanation of the responses in specific countries, some aggregate cross tabulations are shown. In Table 3.2 we see that men and women, the world over, share the same views concerning the criteria by which an abortion should be permitted or proscribed. Age, too, had little impact on attitudes toward abortion, as shown in Table 3.3. Except for the respondents who were over 65, there was little disagreement as to the criteria for permitting abortion or the respondents' general position on the issue. The over-65 respondents were somewhat less likely to approve of abortion under any circumstances, although over 80 percent approved of it if the mother's health was endangered and 68 percent approved if the child was likely to be born with a physical handicap.

We next examined the relationship between marital status and attitudes toward abortion (Table 3.4). A majority of 60.7 percent of the respondents were married, 23.6 percent were single, and the other 15.7 percent were divorced, separated, living together but unmarried, or widowed. Comparing the responses of the married, single, and "other" respondents, we found no significant differences.

As shown in Table 3.5, the more children respondents have, the less likely they are to approve of abortion. The majority of respondents, irrespective of the number of children they have, support the right to an abortion on grounds of the mother's health or the likelihood that the child will be born with a physical handicap. Less than half of the respondents in all of the categories approve of abortion if the mother is not married or the couple does not want to have more children, but the range of approval of from 33.8 to 47.0 percent for respondents who have two, one, or no children drops to approximately 19 percent for those with six or more children.

As shown in Table 3.6, religious beliefs significantly affect a

Table 3.4
Public Opinion by Marital Status, 1981–1984, 1991–1994

Approve/disapprove when mother's health is at risk

Response	Married	Single	Other
Approve	88.2	86.6	87.4
Disapprove	11.8	13.4	12.6
Total N	50083	19491	12990

Approve/disapprove when it is likely the child will be born with a physical handicap

Response	Married	Single	Other
Approve	75.8	69.2	75.6
Disapprove	24.2	30.8	24.4
Total N	49636	19204	12898

Approve/disapprove when the mother is unmarried

Response	Married	Single	Other
Approve	33.0	33.9	33.7
Disapprove	67.0	66.1	66.3
Total N	48961	19054	12697

Approve/disapprove when the married couple does not want to have any more children

Response	Married	Single	Other
Approve	39.7	37.7	40.0
Disapprove	60.3	62.3	60.0
Total N	49331	19157	12768

Table 3.5
Public Opinion by Number of Children, 1981–1984, 1991–1994

Number of children	Mother's health	Handicapped child	Unwed mother	No more children
		Percent Approve		
0	87.0	71.9	33.8	38.5
1	90.0	79.6	37.1	47.0
2	90.6	80.0	35.6	43.4
3	87.4	72.5	29.8	33.7
4	83.9	65.5	25.8	28.4
5	80.7	61.5	23.2	24.9
6+	72.8	53.2	19.1	19.3

Table 3.6
Public Opinion by Religion, 1981–1984, 1991–1994

Item	Catholic	Protestant	Fundamentalist Protestants	Jewish	Muslim	Hindu	Buddhist
			Percent Approve				
Mother's health	83.9	94.0	83.8	91.0	80.0	89.6	96.0
Handicapped child	68.0	80.0	61.3	84.6	68.6	68.7	84.2
Mother unmarried	22.3	38.6	19.8	59.2	53.7	64.1	58.3
Want no more children	26.0	44.6	22.5	61.1	53.5	54.7	64.1

Table 3.7
Public Opinion by Socio-economic Status, 1981–1984, 1991–1994

Socio-economic status	Upper	Middle	Skilled	Unskilled
		Percent Approve		
Mother's health	89.8	89.2	87.7	82.8
Child Handicapped	72.5	72.6	71.7	65.4
Mother unmarried	34.4	34.2	27.9	26.6
Couple does not want children	39.0	39.0	34.5	29.1

respondent's position about abortion with Catholics and fundamentalist Protestant groups believing in more stringent criteria than mainline Protestants and Jews. The other religious groups generally fall in between, or are less consistent in their responses. Among Catholics and Protestants (both mainline and fundamentalists), there was a sharp drop in their approval of abortions on grounds that the mother is unmarried and that a couple does not want more children, as opposed to their approval of abortion to preserve the mother's health or to prevent the birth of a physically handicapped child. A majority of the Jewish, Muslim, Hindu, and Buddhist respondents approve of abortion if the mother is unmarried and if the couple does not want more children.

The survey research organizations divided the respondents by socio-economic status into four groups: upper, middle, skilled, and unskilled. When we compared attitudes about abortion, we did not find strong differences, but there was a trend such that the higher socio-economic status respondents were more likely to approve of abortion on a wider range of criteria than were the respondents in the lower socio-economic groups (Table 3.7).

Educational level showed the same relationship to abortion

Table 3.8
Public Opinion by Educational Level, 1981–1984, 1991–1994

Educational level	Mother's health	Child Handicapped	Mother unmarried	Couple does not want more
		Percent Approve		
1 (lowest)	87.7	71.6	31.2	35.3
2	86.2	68.3	26.5	34.2
3	85.4	66.1	32.0	37.8
4	87.3	67.7	40.0	42.3
5	89.7	75.6	39.5	48.5
6	96.0	85.4	43.3	56.7
7	97.0	83.7	34.9	36.8
8 (highest)	96.0	74.1	43.4	42.1

as did the composite socio-economic status variable. Respondents with more years of schooling expressed greater approval for abortion under a wider range of circumstances (Table 3.8).

In sum, these aggregate data show that over two-thirds of the respondents approve of abortions if the mother's health is at risk or the child is likely to be born with a physical handicap. A majority of the respondents (60 and 55 percent) disapprove of a woman seeking an abortion because she is unmarried or because the husband and wife do not want to have any more children. Gender, age, and marital status made little difference in the attitudes held about the criteria for abortion. Religion, socio-economic status, and education did make for different attitudes on the abortion issue. Respondents with more years of schooling and those classified as upper socio-economic were more likely to approve of abortion, generally, and when the mother was unmarried and the couple did not want any more children. Although most Catholics and fundamentalist Protestants approve of the use of abortion if a mother's health is at risk, or the child is likely to be born with a handicap, they are

Table 3.9
Criteria for Abortion Percent Approve, Great Britain, 1981–1984, 1991–1994

	1981-1984	1991-1994
Mother's health	92.3	93.0
Child born handicapped	81.6	79.8
Mother unmarried	33.9	33.2
Couple do not want more children	33.9	39.3

much less likely than other religious groups to approve of abortion if a mother is unmarried or the couple does not want any more children.

In the next section we report responses on a country by country basis, and then compare the public opinion data in those countries against the country's laws and statutes concerning abortion.

WESTERN EUROPE

Great Britain

There were 1199 respondents in the 1981–1984 survey and 1468 in the 1991–1994 survey. As shown below, the responses on the four items soliciting attitudes toward abortion under specific circumstances were very similar on the two surveys. As exhibited in Table 3.9, on both surveys at least 80 percent expressed approval of abortion if the mother's health is endangered or if the child is likely to be born with a handicap, but only about a third said they approve of abortion if the mother is unmarried or if the couple does not want more children.

Examination of the responses by demographic characteristics in the two surveys revealed no significant differences. The responses shown in Table 3.10 are based only on the 1991–1994 survey. Gender, marital status, and number of children did not

Table 3.10
Criteria for Abortion by Demographic Characteristics, Great Britain, 1991–1994

Characteristic	Mother's health	Child Handicapped	Mother Unmarried	Do not want more children
Gender				
Men	99.4	77.0	31.2	41.5
Women	99.5	82.0	35.0	37.4
Marital Status				
Married	93.9	82.0	33.8	39.8
Single	93.1	74.0	34.0	39.0
Other	93.0	78.4	33.5	39.2
Number of Children				
None	94.0	77.1	33.9	39.0
One	92.0	79.2	27.9	39.2
2 or more	92.6	81.4	35.6	39.3
Religion				
Catholic	77.1	55.6	15.3	22.1
Protestant	95.4	83.8	35.3	38.5
Fundamentalist Protestant	91.5	70.6	28.0	35.3
Socio-economic Status				
Upper	96.4	84.2	38.3	43.4
Middle	99.8	81.5	34.9	38.2
Skilled	92.8	80.6	32.2	38.0
Unskilled	88.9	74.1	29.2	39.0

Table 3.11
Criteria for Abortion Percent Approve, the Netherlands, 1981–1984, 1991–1994

Item	1981-1984	1991-1994
Mother's health	93.0	93.5
Child born handicapped	72.9	65.1
Mother unmarried	28.3	30.8
Couple do not want more children	23.7	28.1

differentiate respondents' approval or disapproval of abortion under the four circumstances described above. Catholics were less likely to approve of abortion than were either mainline or fundamentalist Protestants. Unlike the responses shown in the worldwide survey, the fundamentalist Protestant attitudes in Britain were closer to the mainstream Protestants' than they were to the attitudes held by British Catholics. Socio-economic status showed a slight tendency for lower status respondents to be less approving of abortion in all four contexts than higher status respondents. An unmarried woman seeking an abortion received the lowest percentage of approval among respondents in any of the demographic categories.

The current British statutes concerning grounds for which abortions may be obtained are more permissive than public opinion. Less than 40 percent of the British public approve of abortion for social and for economic reasons, but according to the law, women may obtain an abortion for social and economic reasons, if they are within twenty-four weeks of gestation after two medical practitioners certify that the grounds have been met.

The Netherlands

The surveys conducted in the Netherlands consisted of 1148 respondents in 1981–1984 and of 1008 respondents in 1991–

Table 3.12
Criteria for Abortion by Demographic Characteristics, the Netherlands, 1991–1994

Characteristic	Mother's health	Child handicapped	Mother unmarried	Do not want more children
Gender				
Men	93.3	63.4	31.1	29.1
Women	93.7	66.4	30.6	27.4
Marital Status				
Married	94.0	68.2	28.2	23.5
Single	92.8	57.0	36.6	38.3
Other	92.7	64.5	31.5	30.4
Children				
None	92.7	60.2	35.0	36.3
One	93.3	72.6	40.2	29.4
Two or more	94.9	70.0	30.7	27.7
Religion				
Catholic	93.2	60.3	26.2	19.7
Protestant	87.8	50.0	13.4	8.4
Fundamentalist Protestant	89.3	39.6	18.5	10.9
Socio-economic Status				
Upper	96.6	67.4	33.7	33.7
Middle	94.3	67.4	35.8	37.5
Skilled	93.9	63.6	27.2	20.9
Unskilled	87.8	62.4	23.1	16.8

1994. The responses to the items concerning criteria for abortion are shown in Table 3.11 for each of the surveys. Only the 1991–1994 survey data by demographic characteristics are reported because there were no significant differences in the responses on the two surveys (Table 3.12).

The responses of the Catholics, Protestants, and fundamentalist Protestants are unusual in that the Catholics are more likely to approve of abortion under all four circumstances than are the mainline Protestants. Except for that anomaly, the other responses fit what is becoming a typical pattern: almost everyone approved of abortion if the mother's health is endangered; a majority approved, usually over 60 percent, if the child is likely to be born with a handicap; single respondents, those with children, and those of higher socio-economic status are more likely to approve if the mother is unmarried and if the couple does not want more children. The responses of the men and women are practically the same for all four circumstances.

The Dutch statutes vis-à-vis abortion like the British are more liberal than public opinion. Current law permits abortions virtually upon request and are subsidized by the government. But less than a third of the respondents approve of abortion if the mother is unmarried or if the couple does not want any more children. Interestingly, in the Netherlands, Catholics indicate greater approval for abortion than do Protestants on all four criteria: mother's health, child born with a handicap, the women is unmarried, and the couple do not want any more children.

Denmark

The first survey consisted of 1171 respondents and the second of 994 respondents. The responses on each survey to the items concerning the criteria for abortion are shown in Table 3.13.

The relationship between appropriate criteria for abortion and demographic characteristics are described in Table 3.14. The level of support for abortion is high among persons with different demographic characteristics for all four criteria. And, the high level of support for abortion is consistent with the current statutes vis-à-vis abortion, which is available on request up to the end of the first trimester.

Table 3.13
Criteria for Abortion Percent Approve, Denmark, 1981–1984, 1991–1994

Item	1981-1984	1991-1994
Mother's health	97.0	97.5
Child born handicapped	92.9	83.8
Mother unmarried	62.0	57.4
Couple do not want more children	70.3	63.3

Sweden

The first survey consisted of 954 respondents and the second of 1047. Shown in Table 3.15 are the responses to the items concerning legitimate criteria for abortion on the two surveys.

The survey responses by demographic characteristics are described in Table 3.16. Since socio-economic status was not included, we substituted annual income and report those in the highest and lowest categories. Respondents in the lowest income category, who represent 44 percent of the sample, indicated greater approval for abortion on three of the four grounds than did respondents in the highest income category. None of the other demographic characteristics showed a consistent or significant pattern.

The current law in Sweden permits abortion on request up to eighteen weeks of pregnancy and it is provided free. The majority of the Swedish public appears to support that practice except when the reason for the abortion is the prospective mother's marital status. On that ground only 40 percent of the public approves.

Germany

There are three sets of survey data available for Germany; two for West Germany, one in 1981–1984 and the other in

Table 3.14
Criteria for Abortion By Demographic Characteristics, Denmark, 1981–1984, 1991–1994

Characteristic	Mother's health	Child born handicapped	Unmarried mother	Couple do not want children
Gender				
Men	97.2	84.3	60.6	66.2
Women	97.7	83.3	54.2	60.2
Marital Status				
Married	97.5	83.9	54.9	62.1
Single	97.0	82.7	64.7	69.0
Other	99.0	84.4	56.8	61.5
Number of Children				
None	94.7	89.0	72.6	77.7
One	98.9	96.0	58.9	73.2
Two or more	98.4	95.6	57.2	65.9
Religion				
Protestant*	97.5	83.8	57.4	63.6
Socio-Economic Status**				
Upper	99.0	94.0	64.4	72.5
Middle	97.0	93.4	65.1	72.6
Skilled	95.3	90.6	55.3	65.4

*Comprise 89 percent of the respondents; the next largest category is the "No Answer" at 8.5 percent.

**Based on responses to the 1981–1984 survey. Data are not available for the second survey.

Table 3.15
Criteria for Abortion Percent Approve, Sweden, 1981–1984, 1991–1994

Item	1981-1984	1991-1994
Mother's health	98.1	97.5
Child born handicapped	89.3	80.0
Mother unmarried	40.0	40.8
Couple do not want more children	59.3	52.3

1991–1994 composed of 1300 and 2100 respondents, respectively, and one for East Germany conducted between 1991–1994 composed of 1330 respondents. Responses on all three surveys are shown in Table 3.17. Only on the issue of whether a woman has the right to an abortion because she and her husband do not want any more children is there a significant difference between the responses of those living in West Germany and those in the former Soviet sphere of East Germany. Respondents in East Germany are more likely to approve of a woman's right to an abortion on those grounds than are the West Germans.

The percentages in Table 3.18 below are based on the demographic characteristics of the respondents in the West German 1991–1994 survey. The responses show that respondents with no children, Protestants, and higher status respondents are more likely to approve of abortion on socio-economic or personal grounds than are married, Catholic, lower status persons and respondents with two or more children.

Among the East German respondents, Protestants were more approving of abortion for socio-economic and personal reasons than Catholics, 11.5 percent versus .7 percent and 34.2 percent versus 14.2 percent. There were no significant differences among respondents in the other social groups.

Following unification of East and West Germany, the new Parliament in June 1992 adopted the current law that permits

Table 3.16
Criteria for Abortion by Demographic Characteristics, Sweden, 1981–1984, 1991–1994

Characteristic	Mother's health	Child handicapped	Mother unmarried	Do not want more children
Gender				
Men	98	82.0	43.8	55.1
Women	97	77.8	37.5	49.0
Marital Status				
Married	98.0	81.0	37.8	52.1
Single	97.0	79.3	40.6	52.0
Other	97.0	79.4	47.2	50.0
Children				
None	96.0	79.1	46.0	52.3
One	98.0	78.8	31.2	46.9
Two or more	97.0	80.0	40.0	54.3
Religion*				
Protestant	98.0	81.5	41.0	52.2
Income				
Highest	98.4	73.8	33.5	45.5
Lowest	98.0	81.7	46.7	58.1

*Protestants made up 76 percent of the sample; almost all of the others identified themselves as "other."

abortion if the mother's health is endangered, if she is a victim of rape or incest, or if the fetus is impaired. These criteria are consistent with the public's attitudes that show support for the mother's health and if the child is likely to be born with a handicap criteria, but indicate much less support if the mother is unmarried or the couple does not want more children.

Table 3.17
Criteria for Abortion Percent Approve, Germany, 1981–1984, 1991–1994

Item	West Germany 1981-1984	West Germany 1991-1994	East Germany 1991-1994
Mother's health	95.9	96.2	96.3
Child born handicapped	84.2	80.8	83.7
Mother unmarried	25.2	22.1	17.4
Couple do not want more children	38.2	30.9	48.4

Austria

Survey data are available only for the 1991–1994 period for which there were 1,460 respondents. Although Austrian statutes permit abortion on demand during the first trimester, public opinion, as reported in Table 3.19, clearly does not approve of abortion unless the mother's health is endangered or the child is likely to be born with a handicap. Demographic characteristics reveal in Table 3.20 little variation in respondents' attitudes on any of the abortion criteria save that non-Catholics are more likely to approve on all four criteria.

Now, we examine public attitudes among the mainly Catholic countries of Western Europe, beginning with Ireland.

Ireland

Of all the countries in Europe, Ireland has the most restrictive policies vis-à-vis abortion. The Irish constitution prohibits the voluntary termination of pregnancy. But in February 1992, the Irish Supreme Court ruled that a 14-year-old rape victim had the right to travel abroad to obtain an abortion because "the life of the girl was endangered by a situation of emotional distress that could lead her to commit suicide." As the data presented in Table 3.21 demonstrate, the results of the public opinion surveys conducted in 1981–1984 with 1217 respondents and in 1991–1994 with 1000 respondents reveal popular support for the official government position. While there has been some shift in views toward greater approval for abortion, notably when the mother's health is endangered, less than 10 percent of the respondents approve of abortion for personal or socio-economic reasons.

With such a small percentage indicating support on those grounds, we examine and report in Table 3.22 the demographic characteristics of respondents' support for abortion only if the mother's health is endangered or if the child is likely to be born with a handicap in the 1991–1994 survey. Religion was not included because 97 percent of the respondents said they were Catholic. The responses for the other characteristics show little variation save that persons of higher socioeconomic status are more supportive of abortion on the two grounds stated above than are persons in the lowest status category.

The official position vis-à-vis abortion in Ireland and public opinion are clearly in sync.

France

In the 1981–1984 survey there were 1200 respondents and in the 1991–1994 survey there were 1002 respondents. The responses were not significantly different in the two time periods. On both surveys much less approval was expressed for abortion because the mother was unmarried or the couple did not want to have any more children, as seen in Table 3.23.

Examination of the responses by demographic characteristics in the two surveys revealed no significant differences. The responses shown in Table 3.24 are based only on the 1991–1994 survey. Respondents who are unmarried and have no children are more likely to approve of abortion for personal and socio-economic reasons. Catholics indicate greater disapproval of abortion for all four grounds than do respondents who label themselves "nonreligious."

The current legal criteria for abortion in France (if a mother's physical or mental health is endangered, if she is a victim of rape or incest, if there is evidence of fetal impairment, or for

Table 3.18
Criteria for Abortion by Demographic Characteristics, Germany, 1991–1994

Characteristics	Mother's health	Child handicapped	Mother unmarried	Couple do not want more children
Gender				
Men	97.4	82.6	23.6	32.6
Women	95.1	79.2	20.8	29.4
Marital Status				
Married	96.4	80.7	19.1	28.1
Single	98.0	81.7	31.1	39.5
Other	94.2	80.9	20.8	41.5
Number of Children				
None	97.2	82.2	31.0	38.6
One	98.5	85.0	22.3	31.9
Two or more	94.8	78.0	20.0	24.7

Religion				
Catholic	95.2	75.7	16.8	22.4
Protestant	97.4	84.3	24.1	33.7
Socio-economic status				
Upper	94.5	85.2	30.9	38.2
Middle	97.3	82.0	21.5	31.4
Skilled	96.2	81.0	22.3	30.9
Unskilled	91.8	73.4	20.0	26.3

Table 3.19
Criteria for Abortion Percent Approve, Austria, 1991–1994

Criteria for Abortion	Percent Approve
Mother's health	93.2
Child handicapped	80.6
Mother unmarried	16.5
Couple do not want more children	28.6

social or economic reasons) are more liberal than the public's attitudes toward abortions. The public's responses indicate clear support for abortion if the mother's health is endangered and if the fetus is impaired; only about a third support abortion on social or economic grounds, which would include the woman's marital status and the couple's lack of desire for more children.

Spain

Spain is the first country in which the responses on the two surveys reveal big differences. The 1981–1984 survey consisted of 2303 respondents and the 1991–1994 survey consisted of 4147 respondents (Table 3.25). Along with the changes in the political system in Spain between 1984 and 1991, there were obvious changes in public attitudes toward social issues, one of which is abortion. The direction was clearly toward greater approval for abortion for a broader range of reasons.

We next compared abortion attitudes by demographic characteristics and found that the greater support for abortion in the 1991–1994 survey occurred across the board in all of the social and demographic categories in the two surveys (Table 3.26).

Italy

As of 1978, abortions are available on demand and are free of charge during the first trimester. On both surveys the Italian

Table 3.20
Criteria for Abortion Based on Demographic Characteristics, Austria, 1991–1994

Characteristic	Mother's health	Child handicapped	Mother unmarried	Couple do not want more children
Gender				
Men	94.6	82.0	17.6	31.3
Women	92.4	79.7	15.9	26.9
Marital Status				
Married	94.2	82.3	16.1	29.9
Single	91.2	71.3	15.0	21.2
Other	92.1	83.0	19.1	30.9
Number of Children				
None	92.6	75.6	19.7	33.3
One	93.1	84.3	21.9	34.9
Two or more	93.6	82.2	13.8	26.5
Religion				
Catholic	92.4	78.4	12.9	23.5
None	97.5	86.7	27.9	45.6
Socio-economic status				
Upper	95.1	75.6	19.7	33.3
Middle	96.4	80.9	17.6	29.2
Skilled	93.7	83.5	17.3	27.8
Unskilled	89.6	78.7	13.5	27.1

Table 3.21
Criteria for Abortion Percent Approve, Ireland, 1981–1984, 1991–1994

Item	1981-1984	1991-1994
Mother's health	47.4	64.8
Child born with handicap	25.7	31.9
Mother unmarried	6.3	7.7
Couple do not want more children	5.0	8.3

public's responses show a much lower level of approval for abortion for personal and socio-economic reasons than their statutes permit. There were 1348 respondents on the first survey and 2010 on the second survey (Table 3.27).

Comparing attitudes by demographic characteristics in the 1991–1994 survey did not reveal any significant pattern (Table 3.28).

We shift now to Eastern Europe where we have already seen important changes in laws and statutes following the break up of the Soviet Empire. The responses on the 1991–1994 survey should reflect the changes that have been initiated vis-à-vis abortion statutes.

EASTERN EUROPE

Except for Hungary, survey data for the countries in Eastern Europe are only available for the 1991–1994 period.

The Czech Republic

Following the breakup of the Soviet Empire, other countries in the region also broke apart and formed separate nations based on more homogeneous ethnic characteristics. At the time of the 1991–1994 public opinion poll, instead of a single state of Czechoslovakia, there were two nations. We first report sur-

Table 3.22
Criteria for Abortion Based on Demographic Characteristics, Ireland, 1991–1994

Characteristic	Mother's health	Child likely to be born handicapped
Gender		
Men	66.8	35.3
Women	63.0	28.9
Marital Status		
Married	64.7	33.7
Single	68.2	27.8
Other	54.0	33.0
Number of children		
None	68.2	29.5
One	80.0	39.0
Two or more	62.3	41.0
Socio-economic status		
Upper	74.4	35.5
Middle	69.5	32.7
Skilled	64.0	32.7
Unskilled	57.2	29.4

vey responses for the Czech Republic for which there were 1396 responses and then for the newly formed nation of Slovenia for which there were 1035 responses.

Attitudes toward support for abortion if the mother's health is endangered were not available but on the other three criteria the responses show strong approval for abortion if the child is likely to be born with a handicap and if the mother is unmarried (Table 3.29). Only a third of the respondents approve of abortion because a couple does not want any more children.

Table 3.23
Criteria for Abortion Percent Approve, France, 1981–1984, 1991–1994

Item	1981-1984	1991-1994
Mother's health	92.1	91.6
Children born handicapped	87.8	83.1
Mother unmarried	34.3	23.9
Couple do not want more children	48.3	40.0

None of the demographic characteristics produced significant differences save that single persons are more likely to approve of abortions if the couple does not want any more children (Table 3.30).

Slovenia

The survey results for Slovenia show interesting differences from those reported for the Czech Republic. In the latter, 93 percent approved of abortion if the mother was unmarried compared to 44 percent in Slovenia; and in Slovenia, 70.4 percent approved of abortion if a couple did not want more children as opposed to 34.3 percent in the Czech Republic (Table 3.31).

Socio-economic status and religion significantly influenced attitudes toward abortion such that the respondents in the lowest category and Catholics were least likely to approve of abortion for any of the four criteria (Table 3.32).

Belarus

The public composed of 1015 respondents supports their country's statutes, which grant abortions on request for three of the four criteria (Table 3.33). Less than 40 percent approve of the right to abortion because the mother is unmarried.

The few demographic characteristics available (gender, mar-

Table 3.24
Criteria for Abortion by Demographic Characteristics, France, 1991–1994

Characteristics	Mother's Health	Child Handicapped	Mother Unmarried	Do Not Want More Children
Gender				
Men	92.5	89.5	30.1	47.2
Women	94.5	91.5	28.4	48.1
Marital Status				
Married	94.0	93.0	26.9	45.6
Single	93.0	84.8	32.7	44.2
Other	92.0	89.7	39.4	56.3
Number of Children				
None	94.0	93.0	37.0	56.0
One	93.1	90.0	--	--
2 or more	90.4	87.0	24.0	23.0
Religion*				
Catholic	85.0	85.0	24.0	40.0
Nonreligious	95.0	95.0	48.0	65.0
Socio-economic Status				
Upper	--	--	39	53
Middle	--	--	--	--
Skilled	--	--	--	--
Unskilled	--	--	30	45

*Number too small to include "Other" categories.
**Data are not available.

Table 3.25
Criteria for Abortion Percent Approve, Spain, 1981–1984, 1991–1994

Item	1981-1984	1991-1994
Mother's health	74.9	83.6
Child born handicapped	54.1	73.9
Mother unmarried	16.4	29.2
Couple do not want more children	17.0	31.5

ital status, and income) revealed only slight variations in approval rating, as shown in Table 3.34; e.g., 50 percent of the single respondents approved of allowing unmarried mothers to abort as opposed to 37 percent of married respondents.

Russia

Like respondents in Belarus, the one criteria for abortion that does not have the support of a majority of the respondents is "mother is unmarried" (Table 3.35). Of the 1961 respondents, only 42 percent approve of abortion on that ground. None of the demographic characteristics differentiated respondents' attitudes on any of the grounds for abortion items (Table 3.36).

Poland

There is a big discrepancy in the degree of approval for abortion on the basis of the grounds for abortion. As shown in Table 3.37, only 13.1 and 26.1 percent, respectively, of the respondents approve of abortion if the mother is unmarried or the couple does not want more children, but 73.7 and 89.1 percent, respectively, approve if the child is likely to be born handicapped or if the mother's health is endangered. Demographic characteristics revealed no differences in attitudes toward abortion by any of the criteria (Table 3.38).

Romania

As shown in Table 3.39, support for abortion among the 1103 respondents is strong for all four criteria. Table 3.40 exhibits that single respondents and those who have no children are more likely to approve of abortion if the mother is unmarried or the couple does not want more children, and persons in the lowest socioeconomic status category are least likely to approve of abortion on three of the four grounds. The mother's marital status makes no difference.

Hungary

Comparing the survey conducted in the 1981–1984 time span with 1464 respondents against the one conducted in the early 1990s with 999 respondents, there is practically no difference in the level of approval for abortion on any of the grounds cited (Table 3.41). Persons of lower socio-economic status are least likely to support abortion if the mother is unmarried or a couple does not want more children. None of the other demographic characteristics make any difference on any of the criteria (Table 3.42).

Bulgaria

Like her neighboring countries, Bulgaria's statutes grant abortions on demand. But unlike many of the countries in the former Eastern bloc, the Bulgarian public supports its country's statutes. As shown in Table 3.43, over 60 percent of the 1034 respondents approve of abortion on all four criteria.

As shown in Table 3.44, demographic characteristics reveal no differential pattern save that respondents in the lowest socio-economic category are least likely to approve of abortion on three of the four criteria.

In sum, there is strong support in all of the Eastern European countries for abortion on grounds of the mother's health and the likelihood that the child would be born handicapped. Only a majority of the respondents in Bulgaria and Romania also

Table 3.26
Criteria for Abortion by Demographic Characteristics, Spain, 1981–1984, 1991–1994

Char-acteristic	Mother's health		Child handicapped		Mother unmarried		Couple does not want more children	
	1981-1984	1990-1994	1981-1984	1990-1994	1981-1984	1990-1994	1981-1984	1990-1994
Gender								
Men	75.8	85.1	58.7	74.3	19.2	32.8	21.2	34.6
Women	71.4	82.2	49.8	73.5	13.7	26.2	14.9	28.8
Marital Status*								
Married	73.4	83.8	51.8	74.5	11.6	26.1	12.3	28.7
Single	82.5	86.9	63.3	75.5	27.7	38.1	27.9	39.3
Number of Children								
None	79.9	87.0	61.7	75.4	25.5	37.3	26.3	39.3

One	83.3	86.5	63.0	76.7	15.8	30.7	16.3	35.9
Two or more	70.0	80.8	47.3	72.2	10.2	23.4	10.7	25.3
Religion								
Catholic	72.7	82.1	50.7	71.5	13.3	25.3	13.0	26.8
Socio-economic Status								
Upper	65.3	77.7	48.4	68.8	13.4	29.0	12.7	34.0
Middle	76.0	84.5	57.6	73.1	17.3	32.5	18.7	34.1
Skilled	77.2	87.8	53.3	78.2	15.3	29.2	16.0	31.2
Un-skilled	75.1	77.2	54.4	70.0	18.8	24.9	19.0	27.6

*Number too small to include "Other" categories.

Table 3.27
Criteria for Abortion Percent Approve, Italy, 1981–1984, 1991–1994

Item	1981-1984	1991-1994
Mother's health	90.1	91.8
Child born handicapped	83.0	78.0
Mother unmarried	29.1	24.9
Couple do not want more children	32.2	27.6

approve of abortion when the mother is unmarried and if the couple does not want more children.

MIDDLE EAST AND AFRICA

Turkey

Although a strongly Muslim country, Turkish responses to the abortion items reveal high levels of approval compared to Protestant Europe and non-Christian Asia. On each of the four criteria, over 60 percent of the 1030 respondents approve of abortion. These responses, as shown in Table 3.45, are consistent with Turkish statutes that grant abortion on demand.

As exhibited in Table 3.46, the demographic characteristics reveal one unusual finding. In Turkey, there are differences by gender, with women more likely than men to approve of abortion on three of the four grounds. In a recent article, "Abortion in Turkey: A Matter of State, Family, or Individual Decision" by Akile Gursog (*Social Science Medicine* 42, no. 4 [1996]: 531–542), the author states that Turkish newspapers frequently publish articles that claim women prefer smaller families and family planning more than men do. None of the other demographic characteristics revealed a consistent pattern.

The only two countries in Africa for which survey data were available are South Africa and Nigeria. As shown in Tables 3.47 through 3.50, the level of approval for abortion on all four grounds are lower in South Africa and Nigeria than they are in any of the European countries except Ireland. The relatively low level of approval for abortion on grounds of the mother's health at 68.6 percent is especially dramatic in Nigeria.

South Africa

Responses are available for two surveys conducted in South Africa and, as shown in Table 3.47, on each criterion a smaller percentage of respondents expressed approval for abortion on the second survey than on the first. In the 1981–1984 survey there were 1596 respondents and in 1991–1994 there were 2736 respondents. The demographics reveal that respondents in the lower income categories were least likely to approve of abortion for any of the four grounds. The other demographic characteristics make no difference (Table 3.48).

Nigeria

Less than a majority of the 1001 respondents expressed approval for abortion on three of the four grounds and, as noted earlier, even when the mother's health is at stake, the approval level is only 68.6 percent compared to percentages of 85 and higher in most European countries (Table 3.49). The demographic characteristics revealed no systematic patterns vis-à-vis the level of approval for abortion (Table 3.50).

ASIA

China

In moving eastward across Europe to Asia, we come to China, a country that has the strongest pro-abortion statutes and policies in the world. How do those rules and practices mesh with public attitudes toward abortion? The data in Table 3.51 show the percentages who approve of abortion by specific criteria.

The Chinese public based on 1,000 responses appears to be strongly supportive of abortion on medical as well as personal and socio-economic grounds. With such a high degree of con-

Table 3.28
Criteria for Abortion by Demographic Characteristics, Italy, 1991–1994

Characteristic	Mother's health	Child handicapped	Mother unmarried	Couple does not want more children
Gender				
Men	92.0	76.5	27.0	30.1
Women	91.7	79.4	23.1	25.4
Marital status*				
Married	93.0	81.8	23.1	27.0
Single	90.3	71.1	28.4	28.4
Number of Children				
None	91.5	74.0	27.5	29.1
One	95.3	88.8	31.2	36.1

Two or more	91.3	77.5	20.1	23.0
Religion*				
Catholic	91.0	75.5	21.0	22.5
Socio-economic Status				
Upper	87.8	77.3	27.1	29.0
Middle	91.9	77.5	25.5	29.0
Skilled	93.5	81.6	25.1	27.2
Un-skilled	90.0	72.8	20.1	22.0

*Number too small to include "Other" categories.

Table 3.29
Criteria for Abortion Percent Approve, Czech Republic, 1991–1994

Item	Percent approved
Mother's health	Not available
Child handicapped	95.3
Mother unmarried	93.0
Couple does not want more children	34.3

sensus, there is no need to examine responses by demographic characteristics.

India

Another country in which there has been strong governmental support for restrictive population policies, including sterilization and abortion on request, is India. How supportive of abortion is the Indian public? While not indicating as high an approval rating for abortion as the Chinese, at least 60 percent of the 2500 respondents said they approved of abortion on each of the four grounds (Table 3.52). Demographic characteristics do not significantly differentiate on any of the criteria, save the Muslims were somewhat less likely to approve of abortion than Hindus (Table 3.53).

Japan

Although Japanese law is much more restrictive vis-à-vis abortion than either the Chinese or the Indian statutes, public support for abortion in Japan, as shown in Table 3.54, is high. In fact, even though the impairment of the fetus is not considered a legal criteria, 77 percent of the 1011 respondents said they would approve of abortion on those grounds.

Demographic characteristics do little to differentiate Japanese responses on the four abortion criteria questions, as shown in Table 3.55. The respondents in the "unskilled" socio-

Table 3.30
Criteria for Abortion by Demographic Characteristics, Czech Republic, 1991–1994

Characteristic	Mother's health	Child handicapped	Mother unmarried	Couple do not want more children
Gender				
Male	Not available	95.1	91.8	35.6
Female	Not available	95.4	94.1	33.0
Marital Status				
Married	Not available	96.0	94.4	34.8
Single	Not available	94.8	86.6	50.4
Other	Not available	92.9	92.6	33.0
Number of Children				
None	Not available	95.3	89.5	32.5
One	Not available	94.6	95.2	38.0
Two or more	Not available	95.4	93.5	33.9
Religion				
Catholic	Not available	94.7	90.1	29.1
Other*	Not available	95.4	95.7	39.9
Income (scale)				
Lower 1/3	Not available	93.6	91.6	30.3
Middle 1/3	Not available	95.8	94.0	34.2
Upper 1/3	Not available	96.3	93.3	38.3

*"Other" includes Orthodox.

Table 3.31
Criteria for Abortion Percent Approve, Slovenia, 1991–1994

Item	Percent Approve
Mother's health	92.1
Child born handicapped	89.6
Mother unmarried	44.0
Couple does not want more children	70.4

economic status category showed less approval for abortion when the mother was unmarried or the couple did not want any more children than did respondents in the high socio-economic status (SES) categories. Japanese law permits abortion on socio-economic grounds.

OCEANIA

Australia

Australia participated only in the 1981–1984 survey with 1228 respondents. And on that survey, the respondents who indicated approval on each of the four criteria represented at least 79 percent of the respondents as shown in Table 3.56.

Other than China, no other country expressed such high levels of approval for abortion. The extent of public approval is consistent with Australia's statutes that grant abortion on request. With such a high degree of consensus, analysis by demographic characteristics is not necessary.

The last part of the world in which survey results are reported are three countries in Latin America (Argentina, Brazil and Chile) Mexico, the United States and Canada.

LATIN AMERICA

Argentina

The responses based on the 1981–1984 survey with 1005 respondents and the 1991–1994 survey with 1002 respondents show a lower level of approval for abortion on the later survey on the first three criteria, and no change on the fourth, as shown in Table 3.57. The results for the 1991–1994 survey are reported in Table 3.58. The demographic characteristics revealed no consistent pattern.

Brazil

Like the respondents in most of the world, Brazilians distinguished sharply between their level of approval for abortion if the mother's health was endangered and other criteria. As shown in Table 3.59, a bare majority of the 1782 respondents approved of abortion if the child was likely to be born handicapped and less than 15 percent approved on socio-economic grounds. Respondents of lower socio-economic status were less likely to approve of abortion on any of the criteria as demonstrated in Table 3.60.

Chile

Of the three Latin American countries, respondents in Chile showed the lowest percentage of approval for abortion on any of the criteria (Table 3.61). Less than a majority of the 1,500 respondents approved of abortion even if the child was likely to be born handicapped.

Neither socio-economic status nor income was available, but none of the other demographic characteristics showed any differences in the attitudes toward abortion (Table 3.62).

Mexico

The Mexican responses of 1837 in the first survey and 1531 in the second are similar to those in the Latin American coun-

Table 3.32
Criteria for Abortion by Demographic Characteristics, Slovenia, 1991–1994

Characteristic	Mother's health	Child handicapped	Mother unmarried	Couple does not want more children
Gender				
Men	92.0	76.5	27.0	30.1
Women	91.7	79.4	23.1	25.4
Marital status*				
Married	93.0	81.8	23.1	27.0
Single	90.3	71.1	28.4	28.4
Number of Children				
None	91.5	74.0	27.5	29.1
One	95.3	88.8	31.2	36.1

Two or more	91.3	77.5	20.1	23.0
Religion*				
Catholic	91.0	75.5	21.0	22.5
Socio-economic Status				
Upper	87.8	77.3	27.1	29.0
Middle	91.9	77.5	25.5	29.0
Skilled	93.5	81.6	25.1	27.2
Un-skilled	90.0	72.8	20.1	22.0

*Number too small to include "Other" categories.

Table 3.33
Criteria for Abortion Percent Approve, Belarus, 1991–1994

Criteria for Abortion	Percent
Mother's health	89.0
Child handicapped	91.2
Mother unmarried	38.9
Couple do not want more children	66.2

Table 3.34
Criteria for Abortion Based on Demographic Characteristics, Belarus, 1991–1994

Characteristic	Mother's health	Child handicapped	Mother unmarried	Couple do not want more children
Gender				
Men	88.7	88.7	37.6	66.5
Women	89.2	93.2	40.0	66.0
Marital Status				
Married	88.4	90.7	36.8	66.5
Single	91.6	90.9	49.6	70.7
Religion*				
Income				
Low	91.0	91.9	33.2	61.9
Middle	89.4	91.8	41.3	69.0
High	82.8	85.9	44.5	66.4

*Number consisted primarily of "Other" and "No answer."

Table 3.35
Criteria for Abortion Percent Approve, Russia, 1991–1994

Item	Percent
Mother's health	71.3
Child born handicapped	84.0
Mother unmarried	42.1
Couple does not want more children	66.6

tries. As demonstrated in Table 3.63, they showed high levels of approval for abortion when the mother's health is endangered, moderate support (a majority) if the child is likely to be born handicapped, and less than 20 percent support for socio-economic and personal grounds. As shown in Table 3.64, only religious beliefs differentiated respondents' attitudes on abortion, with non-Catholics showing much higher levels of approval than Catholics.

Finally, we move northward to the United States and Canada.

NORTH AMERICA

United States

Respondents to the two surveys (2325 on the first and 1839 on the second) expressed similar attitudes on both. As shown in Table 3.65 there were high levels of approval for abortion if the mother's health is endangered, but on the other three criteria, the U.S. public is closer to Latin America than it is to Western Europe. Table 3.66 demonstrates that respondents with no children and single respondents are more likely to support abortion on socio-economic grounds, and persons of lower socio-economic status are less likely to approve of abortion on any grounds.

Table 3.36
Criteria for Abortion Based on Demographic Characteristics, Russia, 1991–1994

Characteristics	Mother's health	Child handicapped	Mother unmarried	Couple does not want more children
Gender				
Men	74.0	85.4	41.8	65.7
Women	69.4	83.0	42.4	67.4
Marital Status				
Married	71.0	85.0	42.3	67.3
Divorced	72.8	83.6	43.1	54.4
Single	75.0	84.8	42.4	69.5
Religion*				
None	73.0	84.2	41.4	70.4
Russian Orthodox	66.9	83.9	45.0	60.9
Number of Children				
None	75.1	83.4	40.7	68.4
One	71.4	84.5	43.0	65.9
Two or more	70.2	83.9	41.9	66.3

*Number too small to include "Other" categories.

Canada

Canadian responses of 1254 on the first and 1730 on the second survey show a higher level of approval for abortion than did U.S. responses, as shown in Table 3.67. They are closer to those of Western Europe. Table 3.68 exhibits that like the U.S. and like respondents in most parts of the world, persons of lower socio-economic status are less likely to approve of abor-

Table 3.37
Criteria for Abortion Percent Approve, Poland, 1991–1994

Item	Percent
Mother's health	89.1
Child handicapped	73.7
Mother unmarried	13.1
Couple do not want more children	26.1

tion for socio-economic reasons. Catholics are also less supportive of abortions on socio-economic grounds.

NATIONAL STATUTES V. PUBLIC POLICY

This section assesses the relationship between a country's statutes concerning the grounds for which abortion may be obtained and the public's opinions about those grounds. It assesses the extent to which the public supports its country's rules vis-à-vis abortion and the specific grounds on which abortions may be obtained.

By computing a mean public approval rating for each country and comparing that rating against a score given to each country for its statutes prohibiting or permitting abortion (e.g., a country that does not permit abortion on any grounds received a zero and a country that permits abortion on all four grounds received a four), we were able to correlate the two measures. We found a positive relationship of r = .60 (sig. .003) for the thirty-one countries on which both measures were available.

Table 3.69 describes the percentage of the publics in all of the countries combined who approve of abortion on each of the four grounds stated in the survey: mother's health, likelihood that the child will be born with a handicap, the mother is unmarried, and a couple does not want more children. Table 3.69 also reports the five countries that have the highest and the

Table 3.38
Criteria for Abortion Based on Demographic Characteristics, Poland, 1991–1994

Characteristic	Mother's health	Child handicapped	Mother unmarried	Couple do not want more children
Gender				
Men	88.7	72.4	13.6	27.5
Women	89.5	74.9	12.5	24.7
Marital Status				
Married	88.6	75.3	13.5	27.2
Single	90.7	65.8	11.0	22.7
Other	90.3	73.8	14.1	23.6
Number of Children				
None	91.5	66.9	11.3	24.7
One	89.2	76.2	18.3	35.4
Two or more	88.4	75.3	12.5	24.6
Religion*				
Catholic	88.7	72.8	12.1	24.7
Socio-economic Status				
Upper	83.3	80.8	12.0	33.3
Middle	90.0	75.2	13.0	28.4
Skilled	90.0	73.2	13.0	25.4
Unskilled	83.3	69.6	17.3	18.9

*Number too small to include "Other" categories.

Table 3.39
Criteria for Abortion Percent Approve, Romania, 1991–1994

Item	Percent
Mother's health	88.4
Child handicapped	80.5
Mother unmarried	50.9
Couple do not want more children	67.1

lowest percentages of approval for abortion on each of the grounds.

The biggest differences between the countries with the highest and lowest approval ratings occur for criteria "three" and "four," mother's marital status and a couple's desire for no more children. For all of the countries combined, over 80 percent of the publics approve of abortion if the mother's life or health is endangered, and over 68 percent approve if the child is likely to be born with a handicap.

When we examined the relationship between the countries' statutes and those ratings, we found that the four countries with the highest approval ratings had statutes that permit abortions on request and are paid for by the state. The five countries that have the lowest approval ratings either forbid abortion on any grounds (Chile) or permit it only if the mother's life is endangered (Ireland, Nigeria, and Brazil). The fifth (South Africa) permits abortion not only if the mother's life is endangered, but also if the mother is a victim of rape or incest, or if the child is likely to be born with a handicap. Even on grounds "three" and "four," at least 50 percent of the respondents in countries that permit abortion on demand approve of it on those grounds. China, the country that enforces a one-child-per-family policy, shows the strongest support for abortion, at 75.6 percent, if the mother is unmarried, and at 93 percent, if the couple does not want more children.

Demographic characteristics made little difference in explaining support for abortion as a whole or on any of the four

Table 3.40
Criteria for Abortion Based on Demographic Characteristics, Romania, 1991–1994

Characteristic	Mother's health	Child handicapped	Mother unmarried	Couple does not want children
Gender				
Men	90.4	79.4	49.1	65.1
Women	86.5	81.6	52.6	69.0
Marital Status*				
Married	88.7	80.5	48.6	65.8
Single	91.1	81.8	58.4	75.4
Number of Children				
None	90.1	82.2	59.1	75.7
One	91.2	83.0	50.6	68.7
Two or more	86.0	78.3	46.3	61.4
Social economic Status				
Upper	90.1	84.2	45.2	70.9
Middle	88.5	83.6	51.6	66.6
Skilled	89.0	77.6	52.5	67.8
Unskilled	74.2	48.4	45.2	48.4
Religion				
Other**	89.0	81.0	50.9	67.2

*Number too small to include "Other" categories.
**Includes Orthodox faith.

Table 3.41
Criteria for Abortion Percent Approve, Hungary 1981–1984, 1991–1994

Item	1981-1984	1991-1994
Mother's health	92.1	93.3
Child handicapped	91.6	90.9
Mother unmarried	42.7	36.2
Couple don't want more children	68.7	68.9

stated grounds. The two generalizations that stand out are that Christians, especially Catholics and fundamentalist Protestants, are less approving of abortion on grounds "three" and "four" than are Muslims. Buddhists, Hindus, and Jews, and persons of lower socio-economic status are also less approving on those grounds. Over all, the data show that nations have the abortion statutes that most of their people support.

NOTE

1. The countries that participated in the 1984–1994 survey are: France, Britain, West Germany, Italy, the Netherlands, Denmark, Belgium, Spain, Ireland, United States, Canada, Mexico, South Africa, Hungary, Australia, Norway, Sweden, Switzerland, Iceland, Argentina, Finland. All of the above, except Australia, and the following countries participated in the 1990–1994 survey: Poland, Brazil, Nigeria, Chile, Belarus, India, Czech Republic, East Germany, Slovenia, Bulgaria, Romania, China, Portugal, Austria, Turkey, Lithuania, Latvia, Estonia, Russia.

Table 3.42
Criteria for Abortion Based on Demographic Characteristics, Hungary, 1981–1984, 1991–1994

Characteristic	Mother's health	Child handicapped	Mother unmarried	Couple do not want more children
Gender				
Men	92.0	90.9	39.9	67.5
Women	92.3	92.3	45.2	69.9
Marital Status				
Married	93.9	93.3	45.2	71.9
Widow	87.3	84.3	34.3	59.3
Single	84.6	84.6	38.6	62.1
Number of Children				
None	87.8	84.9	39.3	65.0
One	95.7	94.0	44.1	71.7
Two or more	92.0	92.7	43.2	68.6
Religion				
Catholic	91.9	90.0	43.2	63.4
Protestant	91.8	88.4	38.3	64.2
Other*	92.4	94.0	43.4	74.9
Socio economic Status				
Upper	96.0	94.6	50.0	77.0
Middle	92.7	93.1	44.7	71.4
Skilled	91.3	91.1	41.9	68.4
Unskilled	91.7	89.3	38.3	61.7

*Includes fundamentalist Protestant, Jewish, and Orthodox.

Table 3.43
Criteria for Abortion Percent Approve, Bulgaria, 1991–1994

Item	Percent
Mother's health	92.0
Child handicapped	90.9
Mother unmarried	63.4
Couple do not want more children	76.6

Table 3.44
Criteria for Abortion Based on Demographic Characteristics, Bulgaria, 1991–1994

Characteristic	Mother's health	Child handicapped	Mother unmarried	Couple does not want more children
Gender				
Men	92.4	90.5	60.0	74.8
Women	91.6	91.3	66.4	78.2
Marital Status				
Married	91.8	91.4	64.1	77.2
Single	93.2	91.7	63.6	81.2
Number of Children				
None	95.5	92.9	64.3	81.9
One	92.8	92.3	63.9	77.3
Two or more	91.0	90.0	64.1	75.3
Religion*				
Socio-economic Status				
Upper	100	97.7	54.8	95.3
Middle	95.3	94.2	65.7	80.1
Skilled	89.9	88.6	63.5	75.2
Unskilled	87.3	85.1	59.0	64.2

*Number consisted primarily of "None" and "Other."

Table 3.45
Criteria for Abortion Percent Approve, Turkey, 1991–1994

Item	Percent
Mother's health	83.5
Child handicapped	76.5
Mother unmarried	64.4
Couple do not want children	62.4

Table 3.46
Criteria for Abortion Based on Demographic Characteristics, Turkey, 1991–1994

Characteristic	Mother's health	Child handicapped	Mother unmarried	Couple do not want more children
Gender				
Men	83.2	70.2	55.3	57.3
Women	83.7	82.7	73.2	67.5
Marital Status*				
Married	82.3	76.1	65.2	61.9
Single	87.1	77.3	58.7	64.5
Number of Children				
None	86.5	80.4	58.3	72.0
One	81.8	80.2	61.2	67.0
Two or more	82.0	75.1	67.6	60.4
Religion*				
Muslim	83.1	76.2	64.3	62.3
Socio-economic Status				
Upper	93.6	88.3	65.1	72.8
Middle	83.7	79.0	64.4	66.3
Skilled	77.7	70.9	65.8	59.5
Unskilled	82.6	73.5	64.6	54.9

*Number too small to include "Other" categories.

Table 3.47
Criteria for Abortion Percent Approve, South Africa, 1981–1984, 1991–1994

Item	1981-1984	1991-1994
Mother's health	87.0	79.8
Child handicapped	72.1	57.2
Mother unmarried	19.3	13.3
Couple does not want more children	17.7	14.1

Table 3.48
Criteria for Abortion Based on Demographic Characteristics, South Africa, 1991–1994

Characteristic	Mother's health	Child handicapped	Mother unmarried	Couple do not want more children
Gender				
Men	78.1	54.7	13.0	14.1
Women	81.3	59.3	13.6	14.1
Marital Status				
Married	83.0	61.6	13.9	13.8
Single	75.2	48.8	12.5	13.6
Other	75.1	55.4	12.2	15.2
Number of Children				
None	77.6	53.5	14.1	13.7

One	75.9	56.5	12.8	17.2
Two or more	81.6	58.3	13.1	13.5
Religion				
Catholic	76.8	52.2	12.6	10.8
Anglican	78.4	70.2	19.4	18.6
Dutch Reformed	83.1	57.9	12.3	12.5
Islamic	72.6	42.9	5.4	8.6
Hindu	74.7	58.1	13.8	14.7
Socio-economic Status				
Upper 1/4	94.4	80.2	19.4	18.0
Upper middle 1/4	85.9	66.8	13.8	13.0
Lower middle 1/4	71.6	47.6	12.3	14.5
Lower 1/4	65.3	36.0	7.8	10.5

Table 3.49
Criteria for Abortion Percent Approve, Nigeria, 1991–1994

Item	Percent
Mother's health	68.6
Child handicapped	43.9
Mother unmarried	15.7
Couple do not want more children	28.1

Table 3.50
Criteria for Abortion Based on Demographic Characteristics, Nigeria, 1991–1994

Characteristic	Mother's health	Child handicapped	Mother unmarried	Couple do not want more children
Gender				
Men	70.0	43.4	16.6	31.0
Women	66.6	44.8	14.4	23.9
Marital Status*				
Married	68.8	45.2	11.0	23.8
Single	66.8	43.2	20.9	34.7
Number of Children				
None	66.5	42.5	20.2	33.4
One	66.7	53.8	16.7	35.9
Two or more	71.1	43.8	10.9	21.2

*Numbers too small to include "Other" categories.

Table 3.50 (continued)

Religion				
Catholic	72.3	45.9	19.1	33.2
Protestant	76.2	50.5	13.8	28.6
Fundamentalist	61.1	44.0	12.6	21.7
Protestant				
Muslim	66.1	34.7	15.0	21.4
Socio economic				
Status				
Upper	78.4	54.1	19.8	28.8
Middle	74.3	47.5	14.9	31.5
Skilled	65.4	43.2	16.4	29.3
Unskilled	62.8	35.5	14.2	23.3

Table 3.51
Criteria for Abortion Percent Approve, China, 1991–1994

Item	Percent
Mother's health	91.0
Child born handicapped	94.1
Mother unmarried	75.6
Couple do not want more children	93.0

Table 3.52
Criteria for Abortion Percent Approve, India, 1991–1994

Item	Percent
Mother's health	90.6
Child born handicapped	68.4
Mother unmarried	71.4
Couple do not want more children	60.8

Table 3.53
Criteria for Abortion Based on Demographic Characteristics, India, 1991–1994

Characteristic	Mother's health	Child handicapped	Mother unmarried	Couple do not want more children
Gender				
Men	90.0	67.4	70.0	61.4
Women	91.0	69.6	73.0	60.0
Marital Status*				
Married	92.0	70.3	73.3	61.6
Single	88.2	65.6	66.7	60.5
Number of Children				
None	92.6	77.7	77.1	66.0
One	95.0	69.8	73.6	62.0
Two or more	92.4	70.8	75.0	58.0
Religion				
Muslims	83.3	54.3	64.4	54.3
Hindus	90.8	68.8	72.3	61.3
Socio-economic Status				
Upper	91.4	71.2	66.9	60.2
Middle	91.3	70.2	71.6	62.7
Skilled	90.2	64.1	72.2	60.5
Unskilled	87.0	62.6	73.9	53.1

*Number too small to include "Other" categories.

Table 3.54
Criteria for Abortion Percent Approve, Japan, 1991–1994

Item	Percent
Mother's health	94.9
Child born handicapped	77.4
Mother unmarried	57.5
Couple do not want more children	49.8

Table 3.55
Criteria for Abortion Based on Demographic Characteristics, Japan, 1991–1994

Characteristic*	Mother's health	Child born handicapped	Mother unmarried	Couple do not want more children
Gender				
Male	93.6	78.3	58.1	52.2
Female	96.3	76.6	54.0	47.6
Marital Status**				
Married	95.8	77.0	57.0	49.7
Single	92.6	79.1	57.5	51.3
Number of Children				
None	93.1	77.5	60.0	53.2
One	92.5	74.4	55.0	48.7
Two or more	96.0	80.0	60.0	50.0
Socio-economic Status				
Upper	97.3	77.0	63.1	57.4
Middle	95.8	79.0	60.8	54.8
Skilled	92.2	74.0	58.6	53.5
Unskilled	93.9	77.3	52.3	42.1

*Religion was not included because the frequencies were too small in all the categories save Buddhist.

**Number too small to include "Other" categories.

Table 3.56
Criteria for Abortion Percent Approve, Australia, 1981–1984

Item	Percent
Mother's health	94.5
Child handicapped	90.3
Mother unmarried	79.4
Couple do not want more children	83.1

Table 3.57
Criteria for Abortion Percent Approve, Argentina, 1981–1984, 1991–1994

Item	1981-1984	1991-1994
Mother's health	81.6	77.0
Child handicapped	66.0	58.7
Mother unmarried	28.8	18.5
Couple does not want more children	25.1	25.0

Table 3.58
Criteria for Abortion Based on Demographic Characteristics, Argentina, 1991–1994

Characteristics	Mother's Health	Child handi-capped	Mother un-married	Couple does not want more children
Gender				
Men	77.2	56.3	20.3	25.1
Women	76.9	60.8	16.9	24.8
Marital Status				
Married	76.8	59.9	17.7	24.6
Single	76.5	53.1	20.2	24.3
Other	78.8	62.4	18.8	27.3
Number of Children				
None	76.0	53.7	23.7	26.5

One	74.1	60.5	18.5	28.4
Two or more	78.6	61.0	16.0	23.4
Religion				
Catholic	76.0	57.8	16.6	23.1
Socio-economic Status				
Upper	77.6	57.8	21.6	21.6
Middle	78.4	61.2	20.2	25.1
Skilled	77.5	57.1	16.5	24.9
Unskilled	70.7	55.3	14.6	27.6

Table 3.59
Criteria for Abortion Percent Approve, Brazil, 1991–1994

Item	Percent
Mother's health	86.5
Child handicapped	53.3
Mother unmarried	13.2
Couple do not want more children	14.9

Table 3.60
Criteria for Abortion Based on Demographic Characteristics, Brazil, 1991–1994

Characteristic	Mother's health	Child handicapped	Mother unmarried	Couple does not want more children
Gender				
Men	86.0	49.1	15.2	17.7
Women	87.0	57.7	11.2	12.2
Marital Status				
Married	85.5	53.3	11.2	14.6
Single	87.7	49.5	15.3	15.1
Number of Children				
None	88.0	49.0	15.6	15.2
One	87.2	53.5	13.4	17.5
Two or more	85.3	56.0	11.7	14.1
Religion				
None	88.4	60.4	17.7	22.2
Catholic	87.0	54.9	13.3	15.4
Other	82.7	43.8	9.9	8.3
Socio-economic Status				
Upper	94.7	63.8	20.4	20.7
Middle	91.7	57.5	12.9	15.4
Skilled	87.3	54.1	12.0	14.7
Unskilled	81.9	49.4	13.1	14.2

Table 3.61
Criteria for Abortion Percent Approve, Chile, 1991–1994

Item	Percent
Mother's health	75.3
Child handicapped	40.8
Mother unmarried	6.5
Couple does not want more children	13.9

Table 3.62
Criteria for Abortion Based on Demographic Characteristics, Chile, 1991–1994

Characteristic	Mother's health	Child handicapped	Mother unmarried	Couple do not more children
Gender				
Men	74.8	36.0	7.6	15.0
Women	75.8	45.2	5.6	13.0
Marital Status				
Married	76.2	43.0	7.0	14.3
Single	74.7	33.1	5.5	12.8
Other	73.6	47.6	6.9	14.6
Number of Children				
None	74.3	33.8	5.5	12.5
One	74.6	38.1	7.8	13.8
Two or more	75.9	45.4	6.7	14.8
Religion				
Catholic	76.7	42.4	7.0	13.4
Other	72.5	37.4	5.6	15.1

Table 3.63
Criteria for Abortion Percent Approve, Mexico, 1981–1984, 1991–1994

Item	1981-1984	1991-1994
Mother's health	78.7	81.5
Child handicapped	62.9	57.7
Mother unmarried	15.6	16.9
Couple do not want more children	24.0	19.4

Table 3.64
Criteria for Abortion Based on Demographic Characteristics, Mexico, 1991–1994

Characteristics	Mother's health	Child handicapped	Mother unmarried	Couple do not want more children
Gender				
Men	83.4	56.5	17.3	20.8
Women	79.3	59.1	16.5	17.7
Marital Status				
Married	81.1	54.2	13.3	18.8
Single	83.3	63.2	20.6	19.8
Other	78.1	53.5	18.2	20.1
Number of Children				
None	82.8	61.5	21.3	20.2
One	86.6	65.5	19.9	29.8
Two or more	79.2	52.1	32.2	16.9
Religion				
Catholic	80.3	55.2	15.1	16.3
Non-Catholic	90.6	72.7	28.3	34.9
Socio-economic Status				
Upper	82.1	56.1	16.3	18.2
Middle	89.0	63.4	17.8	21.2
Skilled	79.7	56.8	16.0	20.1
Unskilled	76.3	53.9	17.3	17.3

Table 3.65
Criteria for Abortion Percent Approve, United States, 1981–1984, 1991–1994

Item	Percent	
	1981-1984	1991-1994
Mother's health	88.5	86.0
Child handicapped	60.1	54.1
Mother unmarried	25.9	29.1
Couple does not want more children	24.8	25.8

Table 3.66
Criteria for Abortion Based on Demographic Characteristics, United States, 1991–1994

Characteristics	Mother's health	Child handi-capped	Mother un-married	Couple do not want more children
Gender				
Men	85.4	54.0	28.2	26.0
Women	86.5	54.2	29.9	25.5
Marital Status				
Married	86.8	53.9	27.1	23.1
Single	84.8	56.6	35.8	34.2
Other	83.7	54.7	29.7	27.3
Number of Children				
None	86.7	59.4	38.7	36.7
One	87.6	57.3	33.5	26.6
Two or more	85.0	51.8	24.3	21.4
Religion				
None	88.9	67.7	41.6	40.7
Catholic	84.9	47.5	24.8	20.8
Protestant	88.3	58.0	28.2	23.1
Other	78.7	43.2	22.6	20.2
Socio-economic Status				
Upper	91.1	61.8	39.5	34.2
Middle	86.2	54.9	33.1	30.1
Skilled	84.4	53.9	23.2	20.7
Unskilled	79.1	42.0	18.2	12.1

Table 3.67
Criteria for Abortion Percent Approve, Canada, 1981–1984, 1991–1994

Item	1981-1984	1991-1994
Mother's health	91.3	92.1
Child handicapped	63.7	64.0
Mother unmarried	23.4	32.3
Couple do not want more children	24.3	30.4

Table 3.68
Criteria for Abortion Based on Demographic Characteristics, Canada, 1981–1984, 1991–1994

Charac-teristic	Mother's health		Child handicapped		Mother unmarried		Couple does not want more children	
	1981-1984	1991-1994	1981-1984	1991-1994	1981-1984	1991-1994	1981-1984	1991-1994
Gender								
Men	89.5	91.8	60.9	63.9	24.2	31.8	24.3	30.9
Women	93.1	92.3	66.6	64.1	22.6	32.8	24.3	30.0
Marital Status								
Married	91.5	92.4	65.4	64.9	22.4	29.4	23.1	28.4
Single	89.7	89.4	57.6	56.8	23.8	39.2	25.4	35.8
Other	93.2	93.3	67.3	67.3	27.0	34.6	28.2	31.4
Number of Children								
None	90.5	91.3	60.3	61.6	27.1	41.2	30.0	36.1

One	97.1	95.6	70.0	62.6	23.2	35.7	23.3	33.2
Two or more	90.5	91.6	64.8	65.4	20.5	27.5	20.3	27.1
Religion								
None	N/A	95.5	N/A	74.6	N/A	52.4	N/A	48.8
Catholic	N/A	88.7	N/A	57.0	N/A	20.1	N/A	20.8
Pro-testant	N/A	93.9	N/A	65.2	N/A	30.5	N/A	27.4
Socio-eco-nomic Status								
Upper	N/A	95.9	N/A	66.9	N/A	39.8	N/A	37.2
Middle	N/A	92.2	N/A	66.0	N/A	37.7	N/A	33.3
Skilled	N/A	90.8	N/A	60.2	N/A	23.2	N/A	24.3
Un-skilled	N/A	88.6	N/A	62.5	N/A	25.9	N/A	25.0

Table 3.69
Approval Percentage, 1981–1984, 1991–1994

Items	Combined percentage for all countries	Countries with highest levels of approval					Countries with lowest levels of approval				
		China	India	Turkey	Rom a-nia	Den-mark	Ire-land	Chil e	Nigeria	South Africa	Brazil
Mother's health	81.6	91.0	90.6	83.5	88.4	97.5	64.8	75.3	68.6	79.8	86.5
Child handicapped	68.4	94.1	68.4	76.5	80.5	83.8	31.9	40.8	43.9	57.2	53.3
Mother unmarried	30.5	75.6	71.4	64.4	50.9	57.4	7.7	6.5	15.7	13.1	13.2
Couple does not want more children	36.3	93.0	60.8	62.4	67.1	63.3	8.3	13.9	28.1	14.1	14.9

4

Abortion Statutes and Population Policies

Chapters 2 and 3 provided information about abortion laws and statutes and about public attitudes toward abortion in countries all over the world. It also reported the positive relationship that exists between a country's abortion law and public opinion. This chapter focuses on the relationships between a government's policies or lack of them, vis-à-vis population (i.e., are they pro-or anti-natalist?) and the laws and statutes concerning abortion.

As reported by the Population Division of the Department for Economic and Social Information and Policy Analysis of the UN Secretariat, Table 4.1 describes the distribution of governments' views of population growth rates from 1974 through 1994.

Over the twenty-year time span, the proportion of governments that thought their countries' population growth rates were "too low" declined by more than 100 percent. Almost all of the governments that view their countries' population growth as "too high" comprise the developing countries of the world.

The countries included in the following list are those whose

Table 4.1
Governments' Views of Population Growth Rate, 1974–1994

Year	Too Low	Satisfactory	Too High	Total	Number of Countries
1974	25.0	47. 4	27.6	100	156
1983	18.5	45.2	36.3	100	168
1986	16.5	45.3	38.2	100	170
1989	14.7	45.3	40.0	100	170
1991	13.8	43.7	42.5	100	174
1994	11.6	47.4	41.1	100	190

statutes permit abortion on demand. Next to each country is a summary of the policies that countries have adopted vis-à-vis fertility levels and population.

Abortion on Demand	**Government Policies Vis-à-Vis Fertility Levels and Population**
1. The Netherlands	The government views the country's fertility level and population as satisfactory and does not intervene.
2. Denmark	The government views the current population as too low and would like to see an increase in fertility, but has not initiated any practices or policies to expedite that desire.
3. Sweden	The government views the country's fertility level and population as satisfactory and does not intervene.
4. Belarus	The government views the country's fertility level and population as satisfactory and does not intervene.

5. Czech Republic	The government views the country's fertility level and population as satisfactory and does not intervene.
6. Slovenia	The government views the country's fertility level and population as too low, but has adopted no official policies or practices to change them.
7. Bulgaria	The government views the country's fertility level and population as too low, but has adopted no official policies or practices to change them.
8. Hungary	The government views the country's fertility level and population as too low, but has adopted no official policies or practices to change them.
9. Romania	The government views the country's fertility level and population as too low, but has adopted no official policies or practices to change them.
10. Russia	The government views the country's fertility level and population as satisfactory and does not intervene.
11. China	In 1974, the government introduced the two-child family and in 1979, reduced the number to one child per family. In 1983, the government initiated a national campaign to lower China's population that included mandatory sterilization for couples with two or more children, forced abortions for couples who had unplanned pregnancies, and insertions of IUDs for women with one child. The "one child per family policy" is still the law; enforcement in rural areas is lax. The government provides free contraceptives and maintains major educational programs on the importance and use of contraceptives and population reduction.

12. India	In the 1980s, under the government headed by Indira Ghandi, forced sterilizations were introduced. The government's current policy to lower fertility and reduce population focuses on educational programs that recommend voluntary sterilization and insertion of IUDs.
13. Turkey	In 1982, the government adopted a national policy to reduce population by providing information on family planning. The Population Planning Law of May 1983 legalized sterilization with spousal consent.
14. Tunisia	Tunisia was the first country in Africa to have an official policy directed at reducing fertility as a means of improving socioeconomic development. It passed legislation aimed at providing equal rights for women, abolished polygamy, established a minimum age for marriage, and set the limit at three for the number of children per family allowed to receive government allowances.
15. Cuba	The government views the country's fertility level and population as satisfactory and does not intervene.
16. United States	The government views the country's fertility level and population as satisfactory and does not intervene.
17. Canada	The government views the country's fertility level and population as satisfactory and does not intervene.

Of the seventeen countries that permit abortions on demand, four, China, India, Turkey, and Tunisia, have introduced and implemented policies to reduce fertility and limit population. China's policies, including the one-child family, are the most drastic.

None of the governments that view their countries' fertility levels and population as too low (Denmark, Slovenia, Bulgaria, Hungary, and Romania) has adopted policies or practices that would serve to increase population.

We examine next those countries whose statutes prohibit abortion or permit it only if the mother's life or health is endangered, against their policies vis-à-vis population.

Prohibit Abortion	**Government Policies Vis-à-Vis Fertility Levels and Population**
1. Ireland	The government views the country's fertility level and population as satisfactory and does not intervene.
2. Philippines	The government has introduced tax incentives for couples who limit their family size to two children in an effort to lower fertility and reduce population.
3. Saudi Arabia	The government imposes major restrictions on the distribution and use of contraceptives in order to meet labor force requirements and preserve its national identity.
4. Egypt	The government supports the distribution and use of contraceptives as a means of reducing fertility levels but has introduced no other population reduction policies.
5. Iran	In its five year Economic, Social, and Cultural Development plan introduced in 1989, the government set as its goal a reduction in fertility, four children per woman by the year 2011. In 1991, the government discontinued certain benefits such as subsidized food rations and maternity leave for families with four or more

	children. It also subsidized contraceptive use and sterilization.
6. Nigeria	Although the government adopted a national population policy in 1988, no policies have been initiated to lower fertility rates or reduce population, the stated goals of the 1988 policy.
7. Kenya	In 1989, the government set as its target a reduction in the population growth rate from 3.3 per annum to 2.5 by the year 2000, a reduction in fertility rates from 7.7 to 5.0 in the year 2000 through family planning, and information and services, including the distribution of contraceptives.
8. Argentina	The government views the country's fertility level and population as satisfactory and does not intervene.
9. Brazil	The government views the country's fertility level and population as satisfactory and does not intervene.
10. Chile	The government views the country's fertility level and population as satisfactory and does not intervene.
11. Venezuela	The government views the country's fertility level and population as satisfactory and does not intervene.
12. Mexico	The government views the country's fertility level and population as too high but has adopted no official policies or practices to change them.
13. Costa Rica	The government views the country's fertility level and population as too high but has adopted no official policies or practices to change them.

14. Honduras — The government views the country's fertility level and population as too high but has adopted no official policies or practices to change them.

Of the fourteen countries that do not permit abortions under any circumstances (Chile, the Philippines, and Ireland) and those that permit them to save the mother's life or health, only the Philippines and Iran have policies other than educational programs and the distribution of contraceptives to achieve their stated objective of lower fertility levels and reduced population growth. Both countries introduced tax incentives for families that limit the number of children (in the Philippines to two, in Iran to four) and discontinued other government benefits such as food rations and maternity leaves.

In sum, the data show that among the seventeen countries that permit abortions on demand, four have policies and programs for reducing fertility and lowering population. China's "one child per family" is the most invasive and drastic program. None of the five countries that permit abortion on demand but believe the country's population should be increased has introduced policies that would accomplish that goal. Among the fourteen countries that prohibit abortions completely or allow them only to preserve the mother's life or health, only two have introduced policies to alter their countries' populations. The Philippines and Iran use tax and welfare incentives to reduce population. Unlike the positive relationship we found between abortion statutes and public opinion, government policies vis-à-vis fertility and population size and abortion statutes appear to be unrelated. Of the forty-seven countries in which abortion statutes were examined, China's official policies and public attitudes are most strongly related to its abortion on demand statutes.

5

Concluding Comment

The abortion debate especially in the United States goes on unabated. The courts, the state legislatures, the Congress, the media, and various advocacy groups continue to impose and reduce restrictions, argue the morality and constitutionality of abortion, and demand more government action.

After describing briefly the various historical bases for denying or permitting abortion in different societies over thousands of years, data are presented on the current grounds for abortion in 189 countries all over the world. Of those 189, 16 countries do not permit abortion on any grounds even if the mother's life is at stake. And an additional 54 countries do not permit abortion to preserve the physical health of the mother. Twenty-seven of those countries are in Africa, 17 in Asia, 15 in South and Central America and the Caribbean, 6 in Europe, and 5 in the Pacific Ocean.

Abortions are permitted on request in forty-one nations. Tunisia is the only country in Africa to do so and across the Atlantic, a rather strange trio, Canada, the United States, and Cuba do so. In Asia and Europe, almost all of the communist and former communist bloc countries do so along with the Scandinavian countries and Austria, the Netherlands, and Greece.

Public attitudes toward abortion were found to be positively and significantly ($r = .60$, $p < .003$) correlated with abortion statutes. Those countries that had the most restrictive statutes vis-à-vis abortion reported the lowest approval ratings for abortion and those countries that permitted abortion on demand reported the highest approval ratings for abortion. There were big differences in the grounds for which the public was likely to approve abortion. Saving the mother's life or preserving her health received the broadest approval followed by aborting a fetus that would produce a handicapped child. Less than one-third of the respondents the world over approve of abortion on grounds that the mother is unmarried and 36 percent on grounds that a couple does not want more children. The Chinese public showed the strongest support for abortion on personal, social, and economic grounds.

Men and women hardly ever differed in their level of support, or on the grounds for which they approved of abortion. On the whole, the two generalizations that the demographic data support are that Catholics and fundamentalist Protestants have greater opposition to abortion than Muslims, Hindus, and Buddhists, and persons of lower socio-economic status are less likely to approve of abortions, especially for personal and socio-economic reasons.

We found little relationship between a country's abortion statutes and its policies vis-à-vis fertility control and population growth or reduction. Four of the seventeen countries analyzed in detail that permit abortions on demand had introduced invasive policies to limit and lower population size and growth. China with its "one child per family" maintains the strongest policies. None of the governments that view their country's fertility levels and population as too low has policies or practices that would serve as incentives for growth, even in the Eastern European countries that had been part of the Communist bloc. And among the fourteen countries that restrict abortions completely, or allow them only if the mother's life or health is endangered, only two, the Philippines and Iran, have introduced tax incentives and other government measures to reduce population growth.

Additional Recommended Reading

Borg, S., and J. Lasker. *When Pregnancy Fails*. London: Routledge and Kegan Paul, 1982.

Buergenthal, T., R. Norris, and D. Shelton. *Protecting Human Rights in the Americas*. (1982). Strasbourg: Engel Verlag, 1981.

Callahan, D. *Abortion: Law, Choice and Morality*. New York: Macmillan, 1970.

Cook, R. J. "Abortion Laws and Policies: Challenges and Opportunities." *International Journal of Gynecology and Obstetrics* Suppl. 3, 61, 1989.

Crum, G., and T. McCormack. *Abortion: Pro-Choice or Pro-Life?* Washington, DC: American University Press, 1992.

David, H. P. "Abortion: Its Prevalence, Correlates, and Costs." In *Determinants of Fertility in Developing Countries*. Vol. 2, edited by R. A. Bulatao, R. D. Lee, with P. Hollerbach and J. Bongaarts, 193–244. New York: Academic Press, 1983.

———, ed. *Abortion Research: International Experience*. Lexington, MA: Lexington Books, 1974.

David, H. P., and H. L. Friedman. "Psychosocial Research in

Abortion: A Transnational Perspective." In *The Abortion Experience: Psychological & Medical Impact*, edited by H. J. Osofsky and J. D. Osofsky, 310–337. New York: Harper and Row, 1973.

Devereux, G. *A Study of Abortion in Primitive Societies*. New York: International Universities Press, 1976 (1955).

Feinberg, J. *The Problem of Abortion*. Belmont, CA: Wadsworth Publishing Co., 1984.

Francke, L. B. *The Ambivalence of Abortion*. New York: Random House, 1978.

Francome, C. *Abortion Freedom: A Worldwide Movement*. London: Allen & Unwin, 1984.

Frankowski, S. J., and G. F. Cole, ed. *Abortion and Protection of the Human Fetus*. Dordrecht, The Netherlands: Martinus Nijhoff Publishers, 1987.

Funk, N., and M. Muellers, ed. *Gender Politics and Post-Communism: Reflections from Eastern Europe and the Former Soviet Union*. New York: Routledge, 1993.

Glendon, M. A. *Abortion and Divorce in Western Law*. Cambridge, MA: Harvard University Press, 1987.

Harris, M., and E. B. Ross. *Death, Sex, and Fertility*. New York: Columbia University Press, 1987.

Heitlinger, A. *Reproduction, Medicine & the Socialist State*. New York: St. Martin's Press, 1987.

Henshaw, S. K., "Induced Abortion: A World Review," 1990. *Family Planning Perspective* 22, 1990.

Jacobson, J. L., *The Global Politics of Abortion*, World Watch Paper 97. Washington, DC: Worldwatch Institute, 1990.

Joffe, C. *The Regulation of Sexuality*. Philadelphia: Temple University Press, 1986.

Jones, E. F. et al. *Teenage Pregnancy in Industrialized Countries*. New Haven, CT: Yale University Press, 1986.

Kapor-Stanulovic, N., and H. L. Friedman, "Studies in Choice Behavior in Yugoslavia." In *Abortion in Psychosocial Perspective*, edited by H. P. David et al., 119–144. New York: Springer, 1978.

Luker, K. *Abortion and the Politics of Motherhood*. Berkeley: University of California Press, 1984.

MacKinnon, C. "*Roe v. Wade*: A Study in Male Ideology." In

Abortion: Moral and Legal Perspectives, edited by J. L. Garfield, 45, 53. Amherst: University of Massachusetts Press, 1984.

McCormack, E. P. *Attitudes Toward Abortion*. Lexington, MA: Lexington, 1975.

McEwan, P. J. M., ed. *Social Science & Medicine: Abortion from a Crosscultural Perspective*. Vol. 42, no. 4, 1996.

Noonan, J. T. *A Private Choice: Abortion in America in the Seventies*. New York: Free Press, 1979.

Noonan, J. T., Jr., "An Almost Absolute Value in History." In *The Problem of Abortion*, edited by J. Feinberg. Belmont, CA: Wadsworth Publishing Co., 1984.

Osofsky, H. J. and J. D. Osofsky. *The Abortion Experience*. ed. New York: Harper and Row, 1973.

Petchsky, R. *Abortion and Woman's Choice: The State, Sexuality, and Reproductive Freedom*. Revised Edition. Boston: Northeastern University Press, 1990.

Riddle, J. M. *Contraception and Abortion from the Ancient World to the Renaissance*. Cambridge, MA: Harvard University Press, 1992.

Rolston, B., and A. Eggert, ed. *Abortion in the New Europe: A Comparative Handbook*. Westport: Greenwood Press, 1994.

Rylko-Bauer, B., "Abortion from a Crosscultural Perspective: An Introduction." *Social Science Medicine* 42:4, 479–482, 1996.

Sachdev, P., ed. *International Handbook on Abortion*. New York: Greenwood Press, 1988.

Staccy, J. *Patriarchy and Socialist Revolution in China*. Berkeley: University of California Press, 1983.

Tietze, C., and S. K. Henshaw. *Induced Abortion: A World Review*. 6th ed. New York: Alan Guttmacher Institute, 1986.

Tribe, L. *Abortion: The Clash of Absolutes*. New York: W. W. Norton, 1990.

United Nations Department of Economics and Social Development, *Abortion Policies: A Global Review*. New York: United Nations, 1995.

Zimmerman, M. K. *Passage Through Abortion*. New York: Praeger, 1977.

Index

Page references with "t" indicate "table."

About the Author

RITA J. SIMON is Professor of Justice at American University. She has written extensively on law, justice, and societal issues. Among her earlier publications are *In the Golden Land: A Century of Russian and Soviet Jewish Immigration* (Praeger, 1997) and *Rabbis, Lawyers, Immigrants, Thieves: Women's Roles in America* (Praeger, 1993).

ISBN 0-275-96060-9

90000>

EAN

9 780275 960605

HARDCOVER BAR CODE